C000022762

Kids' Clothes

Kids' Clothes

Making a complete wardrobe from babyhood to eleven years

Lynn Cardy and Alan Dart

Bell & Hyman

First published in 1981 by
BELL & HYMAN LIMITED
Denmark House
37-39 Queen Elizabeth Street
London SE1 2QB

Text © Lynn Cardy and Alan Dart 1981
Illustrations © Alan Dart 1981

All rights reserved. No part of this
publication may be reproduced, stored
in a retrieval system, or transmitted in
any form, or by any means, electronic,
mechanical, photocopying, recording or
otherwise, without the prior permission
of Bell & Hyman Limited .

**British Library Cataloguing in
Publication Data**
Cardy, Lynn
 Kids' clothes
1. Children's clothing
2. Dressmaking – Pattern books
I. Title   II. Dart, Alan
646.4'06   TT640
ISBN 0-7135-1295-4
ISBN 0-7135-1296-2 Pbk

Designed by Janet Watson
Printed in Hong Kong

Contents

Introduction

The clothes your children wear – do you really like them? What's more, do your children like them? Are they from inexpensive chain stores, which force your highly individual child into a mass-produced mould? Or, are they from childrens' boutiques where the fashion is high and so are the prices?

This book has been compiled for mothers who – with the most basic of sewing and knitting skills – can produce inexpensive yet exciting and practical clothes for their kids. The patterns are basic and easy to make and, if followed through, they combine to create a completely co-ordinated wardrobe for children from 3 months to 11 years. In addition each design has lots of variations and ideas for adding individual touches.

Before You Start

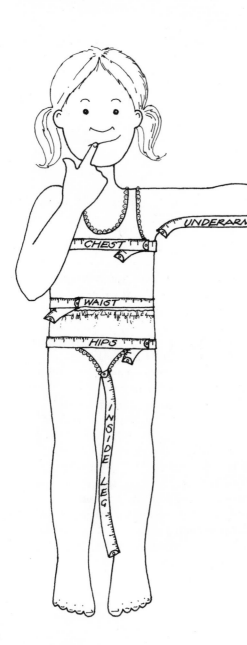

Unfortunately – as far as the home dressmaker is concerned – the average child does not exist. Hopefully, you can make clothes that fit well, will last longer than off-the-peg garments, and will please your children, just by following a few guidelines.

Measuring
First, take your child's basic measurements and compare them with the size chart below, to find the correct pattern size.

	2-3 yrs	*4-5 yrs*
Chest	56cm (22in)	61cm (24in)
Waist	52cm (20in)	55cm (21in)
Hips	61cm (24in)	64cm (25in)
	6-7 yrs	*8-9 yrs*
Chest	66cm (26in)	71cm (28in)
Waist	58cm (23in)	61cm (24in)
Hips	69cm (27in)	74cm (29in)
	10-11 yrs	
Chest	76cm (30in)	
Waist	64cm (25in)	
Hips	79cm (31in)	

Next, note length measurements on your child according to the garment: Blouses, jackets and coats – check back length and underarm seam. Trousers, shorts and dungarees – check inside leg and crutch length.

Cutting the pattern

The instructions in this book include, for each garment, a cutting guide marked out in squares representing 5cm (2in) and showing the correct way to lay the pattern pieces on the fabric. To prepare the actual pattern you will need some pattern guide paper ruled up into 5cm (2in) squares (manufacturers' details on page 127). Select the cutting line required, then mark with a pencil on the pattern paper the exact position of all points shown on the reduced-scale pattern. Join up the points with curved or straight lines until you have a full-scale replica. Remember to include any extra instructions or fold lines. Compare your child's measurements with the actual pattern measurements and adjust accordingly, adding to or subtracting from the pattern piece. Cut out the pattern.

Preparing to cut the fabric

Lay and pin pattern pieces carefully on the fabric using the layout as your guide. (Allow for extra yardage when one-way fabrics, such as velvet or corduroy, are being used. All pattern pieces must then run in one direction.) 1.5cm ($\frac{5}{8}$in) seam turnings are allowed for on all patterns, except where stated in the sewing instructions.

Before You Start to Knit

For good results use the yarns recommended. Yarns from different manufacturers vary quite considerably. If you have difficulty in obtaining them, write to the manufacturers listed on page 125.

Before starting to knit your chosen pattern it is vital that you check your tension carefully; if it's not correct the garment will be the wrong size. To check tension, with the correct size needles, work the amount of stitches and rows required to make a 10cm (4in) square. Pin out and press lightly. If the square is larger than 10cm (4in) try a smaller needle size. If the square is smaller try a larger needle size.

When the garment pieces have been worked, pin the shapes out flat and press lightly. Check instructions on the ball band of your yarn, as some yarns can be pressed damp, some dry and some not at all. One important point – never press the ribbing.

Knitting abbreviations

K	=	knit
P	=	purl
st	=	stitch
sts	=	stitches
tog	=	together
beg	= ·	beginning
inc	=	increase – by working into front and back of stitch
dec	=	decrease – by working two stitches together
cont	=	continue
comm	=	commence, commencement
alt	=	alternate
rem	=	remaining
Sl	=	slip
st st	=	stocking stitch – 1 row knit, 1 row purl
g st	=	garter stitch – every row knit
MC	=	Main Colour
DC	=	Dark Contrast
LC	=	Light Contrast
PSSO	=	pass slipped stitch over
rep	=	repeat

Birth to One Year

1 Teddy Bear push chair suit

All-in-one chunky knit suit with front and back seams. No gaps, no draughts. Cosy hood with lovely little ears. Perfect for Teddy Bears' picnics on chilly days.

Repeat the last 4 rows once more (48 sts).
K 4 rows.
Next rows 1 and 2: dec. 1 st, K to end.
Next rows 3 and 4: K.
Repeat the last 4 rows three more times (40 sts).
Work 52 rows.
Divide for armhole: Next row: K20, slip rem sts on to a stitch holder.
Working on these 20 sts K a further 32 rows.
Next row: Cast off 9 sts, K to end.
Hold these 11 sts on a stitch holder.
Rejoin yarn to held 20 sts and work 34 rows.
Next row: Cast off 9 sts, hold rem 11 sts.

Sleeves (2 alike)
With 5½mm (No.5) needles cast on 45 sts and work 10 rows K1, P1 rib.
Change to 6mm (No.4) needles and cont in g st.
Work 36 (44) rows.
Cast off.

Hood
Join shoulder seams and back seam.
With 6mm (No.4) needle and starting at centre front left side, pick up the 11 held sts from each piece (44 sts).
Work 56 rows in g st.
Cast off.

Ears (2 pieces alike)
With 6mm (No.4) needles cast on 9 sts and work 8 rows in g st.
Dec 1 st at beg of next and every following row until 3 sts rem.
Cast off.

Make up
Follow pressing instructions on ball band. Join 5cm (2in) of front crutch seam. Sew in zip, finishing 3cm (1¼in) down from hood pick-up line. Join inside leg and sleeve seams, sew sleeves into armholes. Fold hood in half widthways and join seam. Position and sew on ears.

Yarn: Of chunky style yarn: 11 (11) 50g balls, plus a 30cm (12in) nylon zip.

Needles: A pair each of 5½mm (No.5) and 6mm (No.4) needles.

Tension: 14 sts and 28 rows to 10cm (4in) square measured over g st on 6mm (No.4) needles.

Measurements: To fit 6-9 months (9 month-1 year) baby; length 60(62.5)cm, 23¾(24½)in, sleeve 18(20)cm, 7(8)in. Instructions for larger sizes are in brackets.

Body (2 pieces alike)
With 5½mm (No.5) needles cast on 43 sts and work 10 rows K1, P1 rib, inc 1 st at end of last row (44 sts).
Change to 6mm (No.4) needles and cont in g st.
Work 38 (46) rows.
Next rows 1 and 2: inc 1 st, K to end.
Next rows 3 and 4: K.

Variations

For an ethnic Teddy, why not knit the suit in tweedy yard? Or in golden yellow with little brown ears – for a traditional Edward Bear?

2 Baby dungarees

Roomy dungarees that really are
practical – button shoulders for quick
exit and entry, plus sweater changes.
Poppers on inside leg for nappy
changing too! Plenty of room in the
seat to accommodate nappies, and
elastic across the back for a good fit.

Sizes: Shown on lay-out thus:
3-6 months - - - - -
9 months-1 year ———

Fabric: 75cm (30in) of 90cm (36in) wide
brushed cotton.

Notions: Bias binding 25mm (1in) wide,
2 buttons, 8 snap studs, narrow elastic,
shirring elastic.

1 With right sides together sew centre
 front seam to crutch, clip curve and
 press.
2 Repeat with top back seam.
3 Machine two lines of shirring elastic
 across line indicated on the back.
 (See 'How To' guide, page 122).
4 With right sides together, sew side
 seams, neaten and press.
5 Inner leg edges: Turn in 6mm ($\frac{1}{4}$in)
 and then 1.5cm ($\frac{5}{8}$in) all along inside
 leg edge and stitch down. Repeat on
 second inside leg edge.

6 Neaten edge then turn up 1.5cm ($\frac{5}{8}$in) hem at trouser bottoms.

7 Measure the child's ankle and run narrow elastic through trouser hem, securing it 1.5cm ($\frac{5}{8}$in) away from ends by stitching through elastic and hem. Cut off excess elastic up to securing stitches.

8 Mark and position press studs evenly along inner leg edge and secure, following manufacturer's instructions.

9 Starting at one underarm edge bind all round neckline, straps and underarms (see 'How To' guide, page 122). Mark buttonholes on round-end straps and buttons on square-end straps. Work buttonholes, sew on buttons and fasten.

Variations

For hot weather wear, make the sun-suit version of these mini dungarees. Just shorten the legs on the pattern and complete in the same way. For little girls, make up in fine pastel cotton, then add a touch of embroidery.

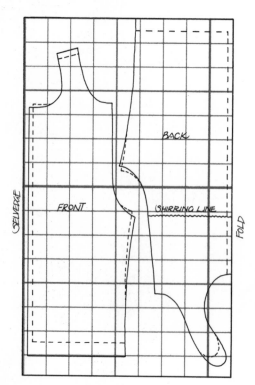

18

3 Baby sac

Warm and cosy baby sac. No need for
blankets; just pop baby in, zip up,
then button the flap for warm toes.
Team it with the knitted hat and mitts
for the perfect winter outfit.

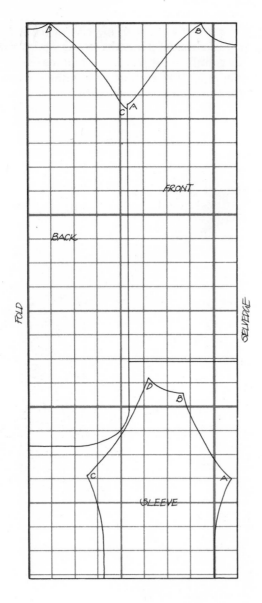

1 Take the two front pieces and pin back a 1.5cm ($\frac{5}{8}$in) turning down both centre front edges. Open zip, place zip sections, right side up, under front edges, starting 1.5cm ($\frac{5}{8}$in) from neck edge and turning under taped edges of zip at top. Tack and sew in place. Check that zip runs smoothly and that top and bottom match.

2 With right sides together, match points A and B on sac front and sleeve front. Pin and sew from point A to B. Clip curve and press. Repeat on second front.

3 With right sides together, match points C and D on sac back and sleeve back. Pin and sew from point C to D. Clip curve and press. Repeat on second sleeve.

4 Bind neck with bias binding (see 'How To' guide, page 122).

5 With right sides together, and taking care to match armhole seams, sew underarm and side seam in one, using a felled seam (see 'How To' guide, page 122). Repeat on second underarm and side seam.

6 Bind sleeves all round cuff, starting and finishing at underarm seam.

7 Bind all round hem, starting and finishing at centre front.

8 Mark and work 4 buttonholes at the foot of the flap. Fold up flap and mark position of buttons. Sew on buttons.

9 Sew tiny hook and eye at neck.

Variations

For winter nights the baby sac is perfect as a sleeping bag. Make it in soft brushed Courtelle.

When your baby has grown out of it, at around nine months, cut off the flap and re-bind the hem to transform it into a dressing gown.

Size: 0-9 months (one size).

Fabric: 1.20m (1$\frac{3}{8}$yd) of 90cm (36in) wide cotton quilting.

Notions: Bias binding 25mm (1in) wide, four buttons, tiny hook and eye, open-ended plastic zip 60cm (24in) long.

4 Baby sweater, hat and mitts

Practical little sweater with matching
hat and mitts, knitted in cotton (it
won't irritate baby's delicate skin).
The pull-on hat has a close fit and the
mitts have no thumbs so they are nice
and easy to pop on and off.

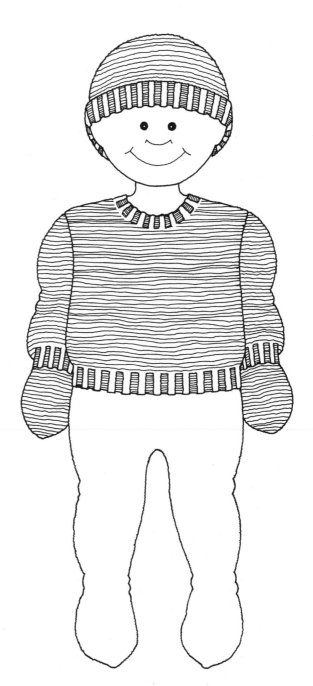

Yarn: Of No.3 cotton: *Long-sleeved
sweater:* 3 (3,4) 50g balls. *Short-sleeved
sweater:* 2(3,3) 50g balls. *Hat and mitts:*
2 50g balls.

Needles: A pair each of 2½mm (No.12)
and 3mm (No.11).

Tension: 26 sts and 38 rows to 10cm
(4in) square measured over st st on 3mm
(No.11) needles.

Measurements: To fit baby 3-6 months
(6-9m, 9m-1 year) old: actual chest
measurement 51(51,51)cm, 20(20,20)in;
length 28(31,34)cm, 11(12¼,13½)in; long
sleeve seam 17(20,23)cm, 6¾(8,9)in;
head measurement 50cm, 20in.
Instructions for larger sizes are in
brackets.

Back
With 2½mm (No.12) needles cast on 67
sts and work 10 rows K1, P1 rib.
Change to 3mm (No.11) needles and
cont in st st, comm with a K row. Work
56 (66,76) rows.

Shape armholes: Cast off 3 sts at beg of next 2 rows (61 sts).
Dec 1 st at beg of next and every following row until 57 sts rem.*
Cont without shaping until 108 (118,128) rows have been worked from comm ending with a P row.
Next row: Cast off 47 sts, K rem 10 sts.
Work 4 rows.
Next row: K (to form fold).
Work 8 rows, comm with a K row.
Cast off.

Front

As back to *
Cont without shaping until 90 (100,110) rows have been worked from comm ending with a P row.
Shape neck: Left side: Next row: K15, slip rem (42) sts on to a stitch holder.
Next row: P.
Next row: K.
Next row: P2 tog, P to end.
Repeat the last 2 rows four more times (10 sts).
Work 7 rows without shaping.
Next row: K (to form fold).
Work 4 rows comm with a K row.
Cast off.

Right side: Hold centre 27 sts, rejoin yarn to rem 15 sts, and K to end.
Next row: P.
Next row: K2 tog, K to end.
Repeat the last 2 rows four more times (10 sts).
Work 7 rows without shaping.
Cast off.

Long sleeves (2 alike)

With 2½mm (No.12) needles cast on 39 sts and work 10 rows K1, P1 rib.
Change to 3 mm (No.11) needles and cont in st st, comm with a K row.
Work 4 rows.
Inc 1 st at beg and end of next and every following 6th (8th,8th) row until there are 53 sts on the needle.

Cont without shaping until 66 (76,86) rows have been worked from comm, ending with a P row.
Shape sleeve head: Cast off 3 sts at beg of next 2 rows (47 sts). Dec 1 st at beg of next and every following row until 19 sts rem. Cast off.

Short sleeves (2 alike)

With 2½mm (No.12) needles cast on 53 sts and work 10 rows K1, P1 rib.
Change to 3mm (No.11) needles and cont in st st, comm with a K row.
Work 4 rows.
Shape sleeve head: Cast off 3 sts at beg of next 2 rows (47 sts). Dec 1 st at beg of next and every following row until 19 sts rem.
Cast off.

Neckband

Join right shoulder. Fold back and sew down both hems of left shoulder opening.
With 2½mm (No.12) needles, and starting at fold of opening, pick up 40 sts across back neck, 13 sts down right side of neck, 27 sts across centre front, and 13 sts up left side (93 sts).
Work 8 rows K1, P1 rib.
Cast off loosely in rib.

Make up

Follow pressing instructions on ball band. Join side and sleeve seams. Overlap left neck opening and catch with a few stitches at armhole end. Sew sleeves into armholes. Make two buttonhole covered loops on front opening edge, and sew buttons on back to correspond.

Hat

With 2½mm (No.12) needles cast on 131 sts and work 40 rows K1, P1 rib, inc 1 st at end of last row (132 sts).
Change to 3mm (No.11 needles and cont in st st, comm with a K row.
Work 20 rows.

Shape crown: Next row: *Sl 1, K1, PSSO, K18, K2 tog* rep from * to * to end.
Next and every following alt row: P.
Next row: *Sl 1, K1, PSSO, K16, K2 tog* rep from * to * to end.
Cont in this manner, dec K sts by 2 each time, until the following row has been worked: *Sl 1, K1, PSSO, K2 tog* rep from * to * to end (12 sts).
Break yarn, thread through sts on needle, draw up and fix. Join seam.

Mitts (2 alike)
With 2½mm (No.12) needles cast on 25 sts and work 10 rows K1, P1 rib, inc 1 st at end of last row (26 sts).
Change to 3mm (No.11) needles and cont in st st, comm with a K row.
Work 18 rows.
Shape top: 1st row: *Sl 1, K1, PSSO, K9, K2 tog* rep from * to * once more.
2nd, 4th and 6th rows: P.
3rd row: *Sl 1, K1, PSSO, K7, K2 tog* rep from * to * once more.
5th row: *Sl 1, K1, PSSO, K5, K2 tog* rep from * to * once more.
Cast off. Join seam.

Variations
Knit lots of these little sweaters in all the bright colours – plus sparkly white for summer.

It's got a choice of sleeve length too – that makes it really versatile.

5 Push chair liner and pillow

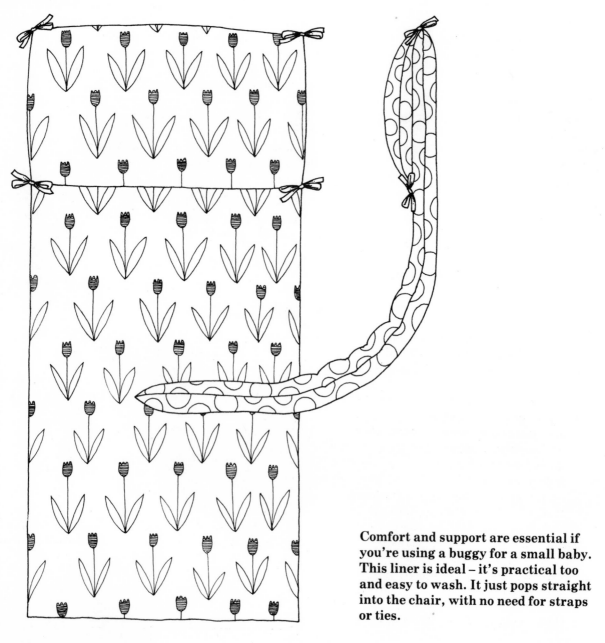

Comfort and support are essential if you're using a buggy for a small baby. This liner is ideal – it's practical too and easy to wash. It just pops straight into the chair, with no need for straps or ties.

four pieces of ribbon at the corners once again) leaving a gap in one short side large enough to insert your hand. Turn through and press. Fill with foam chips and slip stitch the gap by hand.

4　Fasten pillow to liner with four bows, insert into push chair.

Variations

You can make this liner in any fabric you choose, just as long as it's washable. The cover is not removable – you simply pop the whole lot into the washing machine.

Why not select mix-and-match fabrics to ring the changes? Or make one side a warm fabric for winter, the other a light fabric for spring.

Size: To fit normal lie-back buggy.

Fabric: 66cm (26in) of 90cm (36in) wide washable fabric.

Notions: Piece of thin foam 65 × 30cm ($25\frac{1}{2}$ × 12in), 1 small packet of foam chips to fill pillow, 4m ($4\frac{3}{8}$yd) of narrow washable ribbon cut into eight pieces each 50cm (20in) long.

1　With right sides together place two liner pieces together and stitch round two long and one short side, having sandwiched the ends of two pieces of ribbon into the seam at the two sewn corners and two more pieces of ribbon 15cm (6in) further down. Turn out and press.

2　Slide the piece of foam inside the liner, turn in the seam across the bottom and slip stitch closed by hand.

3　With right sides together machine all round the two pillow pieces (sandwiching the ends of the other

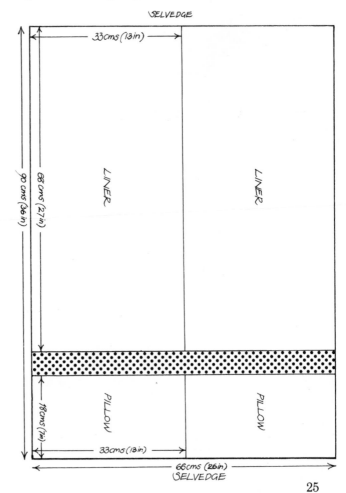

25

6 Baby carrier

For a baby to feel comforted and secure there's nothing better than a baby carrier. It leaves your hands free to cope with shopping or an older child.

Fabric: 98cm ($1\frac{1}{8}$yd) of 90cm (36in) heavy weight cotton fabric. A piece of fabric, i.e. quilting, patchwork or appliqué, 23 × 25cm (9 × $9\frac{3}{4}$in).

Notions: Matching thread.

1 With right sides together, join one long strap piece and one short strap piece to form one very long strap. Repeat with other strap pieces.
2 Fold a 1.5cm ($\frac{5}{8}$in) hem round all sides of strap, then fold strap in half lengthways. Top stitch all round. This forms a very strong support strap. Repeat with second strap.

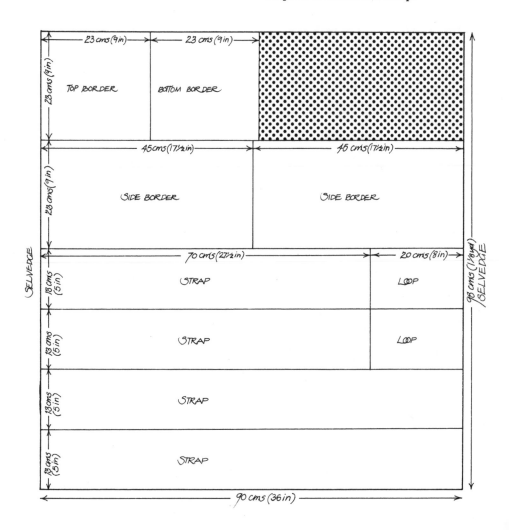

3 Take a loop piece and work in exactly the same way; fold 1.5cm ($\frac{5}{8}$in) hem all round, fold in half lengthways. Top stitch all round. Repeat with second loop.

4 Centre panel: Take the piece of quilting, patchwork or other fabric and place flat with 23cm (9in) edge at top and bottom.

5 Top and bottom borders: Take top border piece and fold under a 1.5cm ($\frac{5}{8}$in) hem along one edge, tack in place. With right sides together pin opposite edge along top edge of centre panel. Machine. Fold border to back of panel matching tacked hem edge to line of stitching. Top stitch down and press. Repeat with bottom border.

6 Side borders: Fold under short edges 1.5cm ($\frac{5}{8}$in) and tack down. Then apply side borders to centre panel in the same way as top borders.

7 Top stitch all round outside edge of completed panel.

8 Pin long straps at underside of panel at top corners, in a diagonal position. Tack down and top stitch into place using an arrowhead shape. Go over this arrowhead at least twice to make it really secure.

9 Fold loops in half and attach to bottom corners in the same way.

Variations

Make the central panel a tiny personal work of art. It could be in patchwork, appliqué, macramé or tapestry.

Remember to mount the centre panel on some strong fabric as it supports the baby's back.

7 Baby changing bag

The changing room in a bag. Roomy pockets for all baby's essentials. Opened up and laid flat, the plastic lining makes an ideal wipe-clean surface for nappy changes.

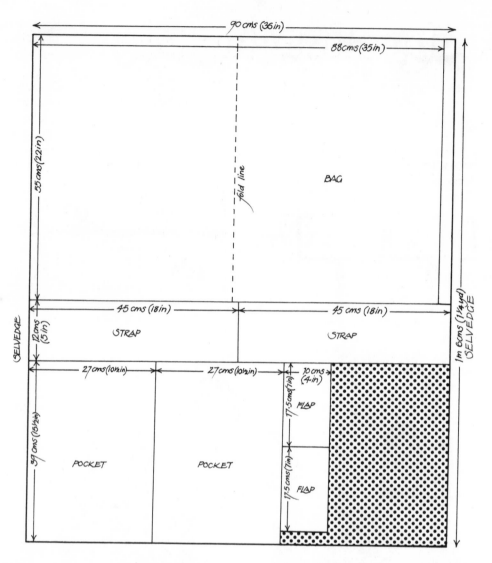

Fabric: 1.06m (1¼yd) of 90cm (36in) wide quilted cotton. A piece of thin shower curtain plastic 45 × 78cm (18 × 31in).

Notions: Bias binding 25mm (1in) wide, 3m (3¼yd) of narrow ribbon to match.

1 On right side of main piece mark the fold with a line of tacking.
2 Neaten all round edges by turning over a tiny hem.
3 Bind one long edge of each pocket piece with bias tape (see 'How To' guide, page 122). Fold and tack a 2cm (¾in) hem all round other three sides of each pocket piece.
4 Position both pockets together centrally on main bag piece with bottoms about 2cm (¾in) away from fold line. Top stitch close to edge all round the three sides of each pocket.
5 On one pocket, stitch two lines from top to bottom to form three divisions. (Make these divisions to suit the size of the things you need to carry.) On

the second pocket, stitch one line
from top to bottom exactly in the
centre to form two divisions.

6 On both pocket flaps, bind two short
and one long edge with bias tape (see
'How To' guide, page 122). Tack
down a 2cm (¾in) hem along remaining long edge.

7 Position tacked top of flaps, right
side up, approx. 1cm (⅜in) above top
edge of pockets. Pin and machine
down close to edge. Sew another line
of top stitching approx. 1cm (⅜in)
away from the first, along top of
flaps.

8 Lay the main bag piece flat with the
wrong side uppermost, and with
wrong sides together lay plastic on
top. This will leave an overlap of
quilted fabric of 5cm (2in) all round.
Fold over quilted fabric and stitch
down long sides and then short sides
with a zigzag or other decorative
stitch.

9 Handles: Neaten the short edges of
one strap piece by turning over a tiny
hem and stitching down. Fold both
long edges into the centre and fold
again to form a strong strap. Top
stitch all round. Repeat with second
strap.

10 Position straps 13cm (5in) in from
sides and 5cm (2in) down from top
edge on outside. Stitch down in cross
shape (see illustration).

11 Cut 6 pieces of ribbon each 50cm
(20in) long. Attach one end of one
piece of ribbon to the inside of bag at
centre of top edge between handles,
and one piece at other top edge to
correspond.

12 Attach a piece to underside of each
pocket flap at centre, and a piece to
each pocket to correspond. Tie flaps
to pockets with a bow.

13 Pull out fold tack line, fold bag in
half, tie bow between handles.

Variations

If you'd like to carry things inside the
bag, why not sew an open-ended zip
down each side. When baby has no
further use for it, it would make a useful
weekend bag for you.

8 Pram and cot duvet covers

Rosie
8lb 8oz
2·3·78

Our Baby

Teddy Bear push chair suit (page 14).

Make a future family heirloom – and show off your sewing talents and creativity with these pretty duvet covers.

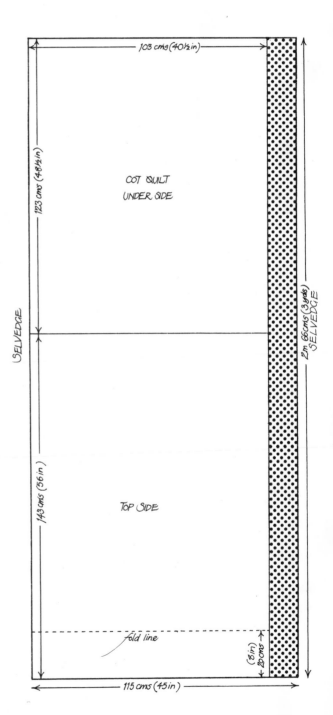

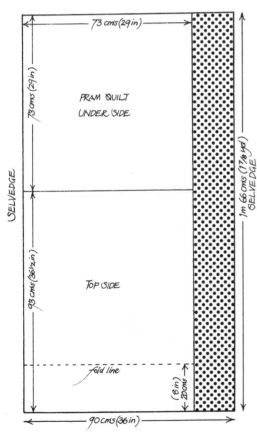

Baby dungarees (page 17), and baby sweater (page 21).

Sizes: *To fit pram:* Duvet 70 × 70cm (28 × 28in). *To fit cot:* Duvet 100 × 120cm (39 × 47 in).

Fabric: *Pram duvet cover:* 1.66m (1⅞yd) of 90cm (36in) wide cotton / Polyester fabric. *Cot duvet cover:* 2.66m (3yd) of 115cm (45in) wide cotton / Polyester fabric.

Notions: Matching thread, decorations as required.

Basic cover

1 Mark the fold line on the top side with a row of tacking.
2 If you wish to, decorate the cover at this stage (see Variations, below, and 'How To' guide, page 124).
3 With right sides together sew one short edge of underside to short edge furthest from fold of top side. Press. Neaten both remaining short edges.
4 Turn flap of top side over (right sides together) at fold and tack down at sides.
5 With right sides together, bring neatened short edge of underside up to folded edge of top side (sandwiching the flap between the layers). Pin and sew the two long sides. Clip corners.
6 Turn the cover through. Then turn the flap through to form a neat envelope. Press.

Variations

These covers give you a chance to display your handiwork over a nice big area. Here are some ideas.

1 Sketch out a stork and baby's vital birth details on paper. Transfer with pencil to the cover. Then embroider it using something simple like chain stitch to outline the design (see 'How To' guide, page 124).

2 Appliqué the sweetest country cottage (see 'How To' guide, page 124).
3 Ribbon writing: simply sign baby's name lightly in pencil or tailors' chalk. Then pin the ribbon over the outline folding to make the angles and curves. Sew down close to both edges. Frame with more ribbon and bows.
4 Nervous about trying your hand at anything too elaborate? Then rule out four straight lines, pin and top stitch broderie anglaise along them. Mark a circle in the centre using a plate and sew individual lace flowers round the circle. There, it's easier than you thought!

9 Babies' bibs

A nifty selection of bibs to incercept the splashes and spills at mealtimes.

Four to choose from:

1 A pretty embroidered one for parties and visits to granny.
2 A useful everyday, cross-over style without ties, it simply opens very wide and slips over baby's head.
3 Towelling and long sleeves, a great combination when your little treasures decide it's time they started to feed themselves.
4 Pocket bib, great for catching crumbs or for slipping the odd rusk into, great for meals on the move.

BABE BIB

Fabric: 50cm (20in) of 90cm (36in) wide fabric will make four bibs.

Notions: Bias binding.

Before you start: Draw pattern out as a rectangle and draw curves at corners and necks with a small plate or saucer.
1 Cut out bib.
2 Bind sides of bib from neck edge to neck edge with bias tape.

3 Bind neck edge.
4 Cut two lengths of bias tape 30cm (12in) long. Fold in half lengthways and sew through.
5 Slip stitch the tape to neck edges, to form ties.

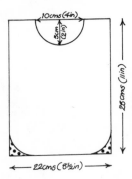

CROSS-OVER BIB

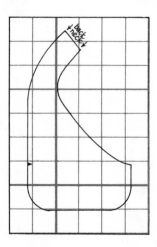

Fabric: 50cm (20in) of 90cm (36in) wide fabric makes two bibs.

Notions: Bias binding.

1 Cut out bib (two pieces).

2 With right sides together, sew back neck seam. Press open.
3 Bind inside front and neck edge.
4 Lay one section over the other and bind all round outside edge, starting at the back neck seam, and binding both pieces together around the bottom edge.

OVERALL BIB

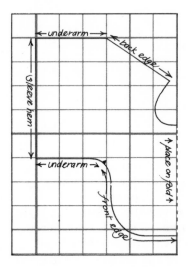

Fabric: 50cm (20in) of 90cm (36in) wide fabric.

Notions: Bias binding, narrow elastic.

1 Cut out bib.
2 Bind straight back edges and curved front edges from triangle to triangle.
3 With right sides together, match underarm edges and sew underarm seams. Press.
4 Neaten sleeve edge and turn up a 1.5cm ($\frac{5}{8}$in) hem and sew, leaving a small gap through which elastic is inserted. Repeat with second sleeve.
5 Thread elastic through casing and draw up to fit. Secure.

6 Bind neck edge.

7 Cut two lengths of bias tape 30cm (12in) long. Fold in half lengthways and sew through. Slip stitch to neck edges, to form ties.

POCKET BIB

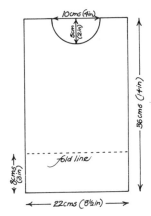

Fabric: 50cm (20in) of 90cm (36in) wide fabric will make four bibs.

Notions: Bias binding.

Before you start: Draw pattern out as a rectangle and draw curve at neck edge with a saucer or small plate.

1 Cut out bib and mark fold line.

2 Bind along bottom edge.

3 Turn up pocket.

4 Bind sides and shoulders.

5 Bind neck.

6 Cut two lengths of bias tape 30cm (12in) long. Fold in half lengthways and sew through. Slip stitch to neck, to form ties.

Two to Five Years

10 Waistcoat

Clever low-cost waistcoats go with any outfit, are quick and easy to make and take very little fabric.

This garment is ideal for beginners to start sewing.

B. KNITTED WAISTCOAT

Yarn: Of double knitting: 2(2) 50g balls.

Needles: A pair of 4mm (No.8).

Tension: 20 sts and 44 rows to 10cm (4in) square measured over g st on 4 mm (No.8) needles.

Measurements: To fit ages 2-3 (4-5): actual chest measurement 68(74)cm, 27(29)in; length 30(32)cm, $12(12\frac{3}{4})$in. Instructions for larger sizes are in brackets.

Back
Cast on 68(74) sts and cont in g st.
Work 60 (68) rows.
Shape armholes: Cast off 4 sts at beg of next 2 rows (60 (66) sts).
Dec 1 st at beg of next and every following row until 54 (56) sts rem.
Cont without shaping until 126 (134) rows have been worked from comm.
Shape shoulders: Cast off 5 sts at beg of next 6 rows.
Cast off rem 24 (26) sts.

Left front
Cast on 34 (37) sts and cont in g st.
Work 60 (68) rows.
Shape armhole: Cast off 4 (5) sts, K to end.
Next row: K.

A. FABRIC WAISTCOAT

Sizes: Shown on layout thus:
2-3 years ———
4-5 years - - - - -

Fabric: 40cm (16in) of 90cm (36in) wide quilted fabric.

Notions: Bias binding 25mm (1in) wide, matching thread.

1 With right sides together place two front pieces with edges together on single back piece and sew shoulder seams. Press.
2 With right sides together sew side seams. Press. (If garment is to be reversible fell the seams after each seam is sewn – see 'How To' guide, page 122).
3 Starting and ending at a side seam bind all round outside edges with bias binding (see 'How To' guide, page 122). Press.
4 Starting and ending at an underarm seam bind round one armhole. Bind second armhole. Press.

Next row: K2 tog, K to end.
Rep these last 2 rows two (three) more
times (27 (28) sts).
K 2 rows.
Shape neck: Dec 1 st at beg of next and
every following 4th row until 15 sts rem.
Cont without shaping until 126 (134)
rows have been worked from comm.
Shape shoulder: Cast off 5 sts at beg of
next and every following alt row.

Right front

Cast on 34 (37) sts and cont in g st.
Work 61 (69) rows.
Cont as left front from *.

Make up

Follow pressing instructions on ball
band. Join side and shoulder seams.

Variations

You really can make these waistcoats in
any fabric; why not make some just for
dressing-up fun? Material suggestions:

1 Real leather from an old coat. Make
   the bottom front squared off, and
   fringe all round hem.
2 For a play version use felt, fringe in
   the same way as above and glue on a
   cut-out felt sheriff's badge.
3 Pretty chintz quilting for girls.
4 Denim for small cowboys, plus a
   spotted scarf?
5 Knitted to make a cosy lining for
   raincoats and jackets.

1 Straight-cut trousers and harem pants

Really versatile basic trousers. Make them in denim or heavy cotton for rough-and-tumble play and schoolwear; or in soft cotton with gathered ankles to pretty them up for little girls.

Sizes: Shown on layout thus:
2-3 years ——
4-5 years - - - - -

Fabric: 1.25m (1⅜yd) of 90cm (36in) wide heavy weight cotton.

Notions: Waistband elastic, matching thread.

1 With right sides together, place two front pieces together and sew curved centre front seam. Clip curve and press.
2 Repeat with two back pieces. Clip seam and press.
3 Open out front and back pieces flat and, with right sides together, sew side seams and press. If you wish to top stitch the side seams for a jeans effect do it at this stage.
4 With right sides together, sew inside leg seam from ankle to ankle making sure you match the centre front and back seams. Clip and press.

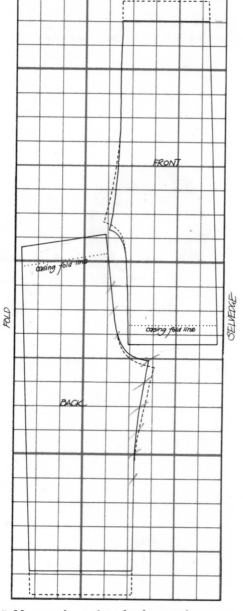

Variations

For harem pants, slot elastic through the hem casing and adjust. This pattern also makes terrific shorts or bermudas. Simply measure up from the hem to the level you want, cut off the excess from the pattern, remembering to add on 3cm (1¼in) for a hem.

5 Neaten the waist edge by turning over a tiny hem and sewing down. Then turn down a 3cm (1¼in) hem to form a casing. Stitch a machine line close to top and bottom of casing, leaving an opening on lower edge to insert elastic.

6 Slot elastic through casing and adjust to fit. Sew securely.

7 Turn up required hem and slip stitch. Press.

12 Face sweaters

Whimsical sweaters – For girls: a smiley face with real plaits and ribbons – touch the necklace; that's real too. For boys: a jolly clown face with fluffy little bobbles on his hat.

Yarn: Of double knitting: 3 (4) 50g balls, plus embroidery silk. *Doll face:* a small quantity of double knitting in pink and yellow, one pink and two black buttons, 50cm (20in) of spotted ribbon, and a few coloured beads, with string to thread them. *Clown face:* a small quantity of double knitting in white, pale blue, navy and orange, one large red button, and 50cm (20in) of pale blue spotted ribbon (for bow tie, if wanted).

Needles: A pair each of 3½mm (No.9) and 4mm (No.8).

Tension: 21 sts and 30 rows to 10cm (4in) square measured over st st on 4mm (No.8) needles.

Measurements: To fit ages 2-3 (4-5): actual chest measurement 66(71)cm, 26(28)in; length 35(40)cm, 14(16)in; sleeve seam 25(29)cm, 10(11½)in. Instructions for larger sizes are in brackets.

Back

With 3½mm (No.9) needles cast on 69 (75) sts and work 12 rows, K1, P1 rib.
Change to 4mm (No.8) needles and cont in st st, comm with a K row.
Work 50 (62) rows.
Shape armholes: Cast off 3 sts at beg of next 2 rows (63 (69) sts).
Dec 1 st at beg of next and every following row until 55 (57) sts rem*.
Cont without shaping until 106 (118) rows have been worked from comm, ending with a P row.
Next row: Cast off 42 (43) sts, K to end (13 (14) sts).
Work 4 rows.
Next row: K (to form fold).
Work 8 rows comm with a K row.
Cast off.

Front

As back to*.
Cont without shaping until 90 (102) rows have been worked from comm, ending with a P row.
Divide for neck: Left side: Next row: K18 (19), slip remaining sts (37,38) on to a stitch holder.
Next row: P.
Next row: K.
Next row: P2 tog, P to end.
Repeat the last 2 rows four more times (13 (14) sts).
Work 5 rows.
Next row: K (to form fold).
Work 4 rows comm with a K row.
Cast off.
Right side: Cast off centre 19 sts, rejoin yarn to rem 18 (19) sts and K to end.
Next row: P.
Next row: K2 tog, K to end.
Repeat the last two rows four more times (13 (14) sts).
Work 5 rows.
Cast off.

Sleeves (2 alike)

With 3½mm (No.9) needles cast on 35 (39) sts and work 12 rows K1, P1 rib.
Change to 4mm (No.8) needles and cont in st st, comm with a K row.
Inc 1 st at beg and end of next and every following 10th row until there are 47 (53) sts on the needle.
Cont without shaping until 76 (88) rows have been worked from comm.
Shape sleeve head: Cast off 3 sts at beg of next two rows (41 (47) sts).
Next row: K2 tog, K to end.
Next row: P2 tog, P to end.
Next row: K.
Next row: P.
2-3 size only: Repeat the last 4 rows three more times (33 sts).
Both sizes: Dec 1 st at beg of next and every following row until 15 sts rem.
Cast off.

Neckband

Join right shoulder. Fold back and sew down both hems of left shoulder opening.
With 3½mm (No.9) needle, and starting at fold of opening, pick up 32 sts across back neck, 12 sts down right side of neck, 19 sts across centre front, and 12 sts up left side (75 sts).
Work 10 rows K1, P1 rib.
Cast off loosely in rib.

Make up

Follow pressing instructions on ball band. Join sides and sleeve seams. Overlap left front opening and catch with a few stitches at armhole end. Sew sleeves into armholes. Make three buttonhole covered loops on front opening edge and sew buttons on back to correspond.

To make faces

Doll face: With 4mm (No.8) needles and pink wool cast on 16 sts and cont in st st, comm with a K row.
Work 2 rows.

Inc 1 st at beg of next and every following row until there are 32 sts on the
needle.
Work 12 rows*.
Dec 1 st at beg of next and every following row until 16 sts rem.
Cast off.
Sew face to jumper. Take a skein of
yellow wool and plait both ends, leaving
enough in the middle for the top of the
head. Tie bows of spotted ribbon round
ends. Sew to head, making a stitched
parting. Sew buttons in place for nose
and eyes.
Embroider mouth in chain stitch (see
'How To' guide, page 124).
String a few beads for necklace and sew
to sweater.
Clown face: Use white wool. As doll face
to *. Change to pale blue wool and cont
in g st, dec 1 st at beg and end of every
following row until 2 sts rem.
Cast off.
Sew face and hat to sweater. Take two
bundles of orange wool and sew strands
together and to sweater for hair. Sew
button on for nose. Embroider mouth
and eyes in chain stitch. Make two
bobbles in navy and sew to hat. Make a
bow from ribbon and sew on for bow tie.

Variations
Lots of scope for different decorations
with the clown face. But why not make a
really special sweater and mirror your
child's face? Match hair colour and
style. Match eye colour and expression,
if you can!

13 Play dungarees, sun suit and dress

Play dungarees with a shapely top –
deep curving neck and armholes. Ties
at back allow for growth; no button
holes or zips to tackle. Roomy
gathered trousers for lots of active
play. Shorten the legs and it's a sun
suit, or add a skirt to make a pretty
pinafore dress.

*Face sweaters (page 45), harem pants
(page 43), and shirred-top skirt (page
64).*

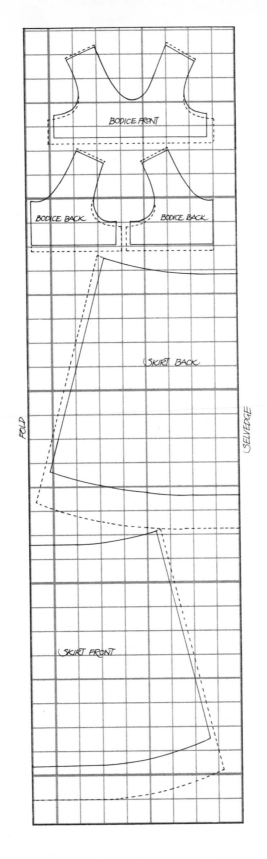

Sizes: Shown on layout thus:

2-3 years ———

4-5 years - - - - -

Fabric: *2-3 years:* 2m (2¼yd) of 90cm (36in) wide cotton fabric. *4-5 years:* 2.20m (2½yd) of 90cm (36in) wide cotton fabric.

Notions: Matching thread.

1 Take the two back bodice pieces and, with right sides together, sew to front bodice piece across one shoulder, then across the second shoulder. Press open. Repeat with second set of back and front bodice pieces.

2 Open both these pieces out flat and with right sides together lay one piece exactly on top of the other.

3 In one movement right round sew a 1.5cm (⅝in) seam up left back opening, round neck and down right back opening. Clip and trim seam allowance.

Play dungarees and sun suit (page 48), loose shirt (page 71), and tee shirt (page 60).

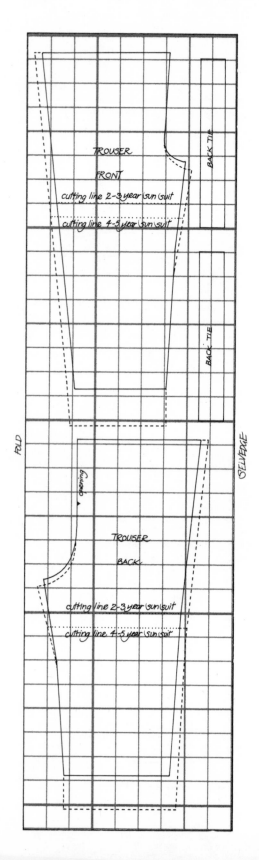

4 Sew armhole edges in the same way, but leave side seams unsewn. Clip and trim seam allowance.

5 Turn bodice right side out by pulling backs through shoulders. Press all round seams. With right sides together, sew front and back side seams in one. Clip and press.

6 Take trouser fronts and, with right sides together, sew centre front curved seam. Clip and press. Repeat with back seam but finish the seam 6cm (2½in) away from top edge for opening. Clip and press seam. Press back a 1.5cm (⅝in) turning at opening and top stitch down.

7 With right sides together match front and back trousers and sew side seams. Press.

8 With right sides together, and taking care to match centre front and centre back seams, new inside leg seam in one. Clip and press.

9 Run two lines of gathering round top of dungarees. With right sides together, pin one layer of bodice to dungarees, matching side seams, centre front and centre back opening. Draw up gathering to fit, pin and sew.

10 Press seam towards bodice. On unsewn layer of bodice turn under a 1.5cm (⅝in) hem and press. Slip stitch pressed edge to previous sewing line on inside of bodice.

11 Neaten trouser bottoms then turn up a 1.5cm (⅝in) hem leaving a gap through which elastic is inserted. Run elastic through hem, adjust to fit and sew ends securely.

12 Take one of the ties and neaten the short ends. Then fold the two long edges towards the centre and press. Fold in half again and top stitch through. Repeat with three remaining ties.

13 Attach ties by pinning two to each bodice at the top and bottom of the opening and top stitching in place with a cross pattern. Tie in bows.

Variations
Make the pinafore version thus:

1 Take back skirt pieces and with right sides together, sew centre back seam, but leave seam unsewn 6cm (2½in) from top edge. Press seam. Press back seam allowance at opening and top stitch round opening.
2 With right sides together match front skirt to back and sew side seams. Press.
3 Attach skirt to bodice in the same way as dungarees.
4 Sew on ties and turn up the hem as required.

14 Monogram jacket

A cuddly monogram jacket, that is very easy to knit. It would make a really lovely personalized gift for any child.

next 2 rows (43 (47) sts).
Dec 1 st at beg of next and every following row until 39 (41) sts rem.
Cont without shaping until 64 (74) rows have been worked from comm.
Shape shoulders: Cast off 9 (10) sts at beg of next 2 rows.
Cast off rem 21 sts.

Left front

With 5½mm (No.5) needles cast on 23 (25) sts and work 8 rows K1, P1 rib.
Change to 6mm (No.4) needles and cont in st st, comm with a K row.
Work 28 (38) rows.
Shape armhole: Next row: Cast off 3 sts, K to end.
Next row: P.
Next row: K2 tog, K to end.
Repeat the last 2 rows until 18 (19) sts rem.
Cont without shaping until 55 (65) rows have been worked from comm, ending with a K row.
Shape neck: Next row: Cast off 6 sts, P to end.
Next row: K.
Next row: P2 tog, P to end.
Repeat the last 2 rows two more times (9 (10) sts).
Work 2 rows.
Cast off.

Right front

With 5½mm (No.5) needles cast on 23 (25) sts and work 8 rows K1, P1 rib.
Change to 6mm (No.4) needles and cont in st st, comm with a K row.
Work 29 (39) rows.
Shape armhole: Next row: Cast off 3 sts, P to end.
Next row: K.
Next row: P2 tog, P to end.
Repeat the last 2 rows until 18 (19) sts rem.
Cont without shaping until 54 (64) rows have been worked from comm, ending with a P row.

Yarn: Of chunky style yarn: 7 (8) 50g balls, plus a small amount of contrast yarn, plus five 2.5cm (1in) buttons in contrast colour.

Needles: A pair each of 5½mm (No.5) and 6mm (No.4).

Tension: 15 sts and 18 rows to 10cm (4in) square measured over st st on 6mm (No.4) needles.

Measurements: To fit ages 2-3 (4-5): actual chest measurement 66(71)cm, 26(28)in; length 35(40)cm, 14(16)in; sleeve seam 25(29)cm, 10(11½)in. Instructions for larger sizes are in brackets.

Back

With 5½mm (No.5) needles cast on 49 (53) sts and work 8 rows K1, P1 rib.
Change to 6mm (No.4) needles and cont in st st, comm with a K row.
Work 28 (38) rows.
Shape armholes: Cast off 3 sts, at beg of

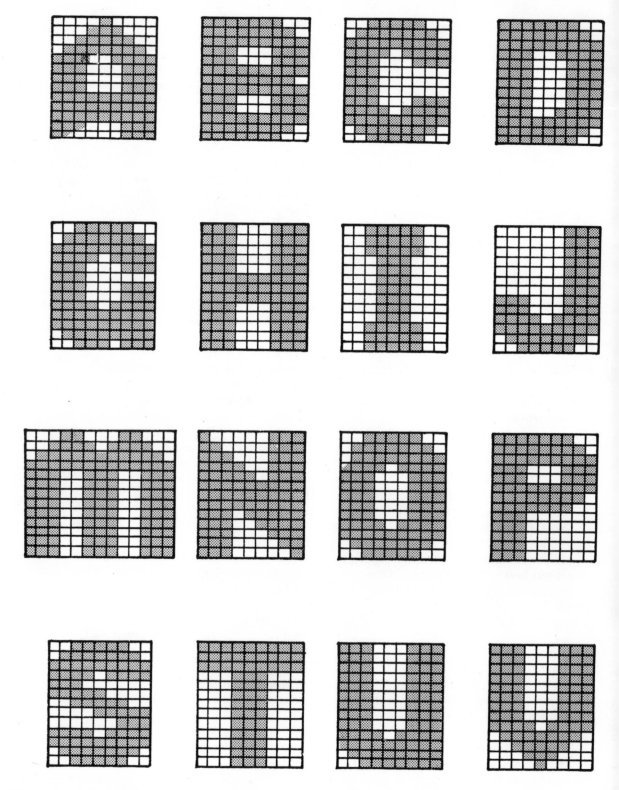

54

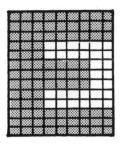
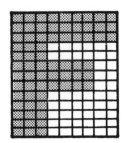

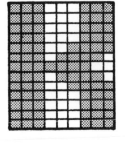
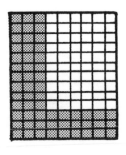
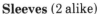

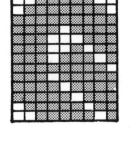
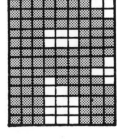

Shape neck: Next row: Cast off 6 sts, K to end.

Next row: P.

Next row: K2 tog, K to end.

Repeat the last 2 rows two more times (9 (10) sts).

Work 3 rows.

Cast off.

Sleeves (2 alike)

With 5½mm (No.5) needles cast on 27 (31) sts and work 8 rows K1, P1 rib.

Change to 6mm (No.4) needles and cont in st st, comm with a K row.

Work 4 rows.

Inc 1 st at beg and end of next and every following 8th (10th) row until there are 35 (39) sts on needle.

Cont without shaping until 46 (56) rows have been worked from comm.

Shape sleeve head: Cast off 3 sts at beg of next 2 rows (29 (33) sts).

Dec 1 st at beg of next and every following row until 11 (19) sts rem.

2-3 year size only: Cast off.

4-5 year size only: Dec 1 st at beg and end of next 4 rows (11 sts).

Cast off.

Button band

With 5½mm (No.5) needles cast on 8 sts and cont in g st.

Work 84 (98) rows.

Cast off.

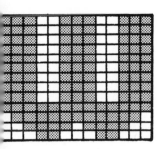
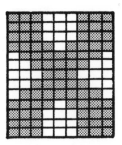
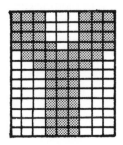
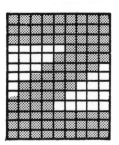

Buttonhole band

With 5½mm (No.5) needles cast on 8 sts and cont in g st.
Work 6 rows.
7th row: K3, cast off 2 sts, K3.
8th row: K3, cast on 2 sts, K3.
Work 16 (20) rows.
Repeat the last 18 (22) rows three more times, then the 7th and 8th rows once more (5 buttonholes).
Work 6 (4) rows.
Cast off.

Collar

With 5½mm (No.5) needles cast on 3 sts and cont in g st.
Work 3 rows.
Inc 1 st at beg of next and every following alt row until there are 15 sts on the needle.
Cont without shaping until 84 rows have been worked from comm.
Dec 1 st at beg of next and every following alt row until 3 sts rem.
Cast off.

Pockets (2 alike)

With 6mm (No.4) needles cast on 17 sts and cont in st st, comm with a K row.
Work 4 rows.
Choose the initial and examine it on pattern chart.
Work initial thus: Next row: K4 (M and W initials K2) – then K 1st row of pattern, working stitches shown as shaded squares in contrast yarn and reading from right to left – K4 (M and W initials K2) in original yarn.
Next row: P4 (M and W initials P2) – then P 2nd row of pattern reading from left to right – P4 (M and W initials P2).
Cont in this manner according to chosen initial until all 13 rows of pattern have been worked.
Next row: P.
Work 6 rows g st.
Cast off.

Make up

Follow pressing instructions on ball band. Join shoulder seams. Join side and sleeve seams. Sew sleeves into armholes. Sew button and buttonhole bands to fronts. Sew shaped edge of collar to neck. Position and sew on pockets. Position and sew on buttons.

Variations

Give the jacket a Stateside look by adding stripes on the sleeves to match the colour of the initials, or by working the front bands and collar in a contrast colour.

15 Activity aprons

And to keep it all clean – a cover-up that really does! Decorate the activity aprons to match your little monster's favourite hobby. Paint on their names or pastimes. Why not let them paint it themselves?

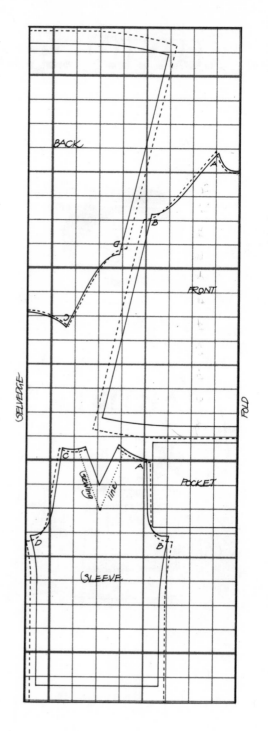

Sizes: Shown on layout thus:
2-3 years ——
4-5 years - - - - -

Fabric: 1.50m (1¾yd) of 90cm (36in) wide washable cotton fabric.

Notions: Bias binding 25mm (1in) wide, matching thread.

1 Take pocket piece and hem 1.5cm (⅝in) all round, sew top seam and tack three remaining sides. Position in centre on front piece of apron and top stitch down on three tacked sides. Sew lines from top to bottom of pocket, making divisions suitable for a variety of objects, e.g. brushes, pencils etc. Decorate at this stage.
2 With right sides together sew darts as indicated by sewing line at sleeve top. Press open.
3 With right sides together match points A and B on apron front to points A and B on sleeve front. Sew between the two points. Clip curve

and press. Repeat with second
sleeve.

4 With right sides together repeat with
points C and D on apron back and
sleeve back. Clip curve and press.
Repeat with second sleeve.

5 With right sides together, and taking
care to match armhole seams, sew
side seams and underarm seams in
one – from wrist to hem.

6 Fold under a 1.5cm ($\frac{5}{8}$in) hem down
centre back edges and sew down.
Press.

7 Bind neck edge with bias binding
(see 'How To' guide, page 122).

8 Cut two pieces of bias binding 50cm
(20in) long, fold in half lengthways
and top stitch through. Slip stitch
securely to underside of back neck
openings on each side to form ties.
Tie in a bow.

9 Neaten cuff edges with a tiny hem,
then turn up a 2cm ($\frac{3}{4}$in) hem and
stitch down, leaving an opening to
insert elastic. Thread through
elastic, adjust to fit and secure.

10 Hem as desired.

Variations

Using 'paint-on' fabric dyes you can
jolly up a plain apron. Block out your
child's name lightly in pencil, either
freehand or using a stencil, then fill in
with dye.

If you don't mind the mess, the
children could paint on their own
names, or brightly coloured pictures.

16 Tee shirt and sweat shirt

Basic cotton knit tee and sweat shirts. The tee shirt has a closely fitting neck with button fastening. The sweat shirt has deep raglan sleeves for ease of movement.

A. TEE SHIRT

Yarn: Of No.3 cotton: 3 (4) 50g balls, plus three shirt buttons.

Needles: A pair each of 2½mm (No.12) and 3mm (No.11) needles.

Tension: 26 sts and 38 rows to 10cm (4in) square measured over st st on 3mm (No.11) needles.

Measurements: To fit ages 2-3 (4-5): actual chest measurement 66(71)cm, 26(28)in; length 35(40)cm, 14(16)in. Instructions for larger sizes are in brackets.

Back

With 2½mm (No.12) needles cast on 85 (91) sts and work 10 rows K1, P1 rib. Change to 3mm (No.11) needles and cont in st st, comm with a K row. Work 66 (80) rows.
Shape armholes: Cast off 3 sts at beg of next 2 rows (79 (85) sts).

Dec 1 st at beg of next and every following row until 69 (71) sts rem*.
Continue without shaping until 134 (150) rows have been worked from comm.
Next row: Cast off 53 (55) sts, K rem 16 (16) sts.
Work 4 rows.
Next row: K (to form fold).
Work 8 rows comm with a K row.
Cast off.

Front
As back to *.
Cont without shaping until 114 (130) rows have been worked from comm, ending with a P row.
Divide for neck: Left side: Next row: K21 (21), slip rem sts (48 (50)) on to a stitch holder.
Next row: P.
Next row: K.
Next row: P2 tog, P to end.
Repeat the last 2 rows four more times (16 (16) sts).
Work 9 rows.

Next row: K (to form fold).
Work 4 rows comm with a K row.
Cast off.
Right side: Cast off centre 27 (29) sts, rejoin yarn to rem 21 (21) sts and K to end.
Next row: P.
Next row: K2 tog, K to end.
Repeat the last 2 rows four more times (16 (16) sts).
Work 9 rows.
Cast off.

Sleeves (2 alike)
With 2½mm (No.12) needles cast on 59 (67) sts and work 10 rows K1, P1 rib.
Change to 3mm (No.11) needles and cont in st st, comm with a K row.
Work 10 rows.
Shape sleeve head: Cast off 3 sts at beg of next 2 rows (53 (61) sts).
Next row: K2 tog, K to end.
Next row: P2 tog, P to end.
Next row: K.
Next row: P.
Repeat the last 4 rows five (two) more times (41 (55) sts).
Dec 1 st at beg of next and every following row until 27 sts rem.
Cast off.

Neckband
Join right shoulder. Fold back and sew down both hems of left shoulder opening.
With 2½mm (No.12) needle and starting at fold of opening, pick up 40 (42) sts across back neck, 15 sts down right side of neck, 27 (29) sts across centre, and 15 sts up left side of neck (97 (101) sts).
Work 8 rows K1, P1 rib.
Cast off loosely in rib.

Make up
Follow pressing instructions on ball band. Join side and sleeve seams. Overlap left front opening and catch with a few stitches at armhole end. Sew sleeves

into armholes. Make three buttonhole covered loops on front opening edge, and sew on buttons on back to correspond.

B. SWEATSHIRT

Yarn: Of No.3 cotton 4 (5) 50g balls, plus one shirt button.

Needles: A pair each of 2½mm (No.12) and 3mm (No.11).

Tension: 26 sts and 38 rows to 10cm (4in) square measured over st st on 3mm (No.11) needles.

Measurements: To fit ages 2-3 (4-5): actual chest measurement 66(71)cm, 26(28)in; length 35(40)cm, 14(16)in; sleeve seam 25(29)cm, 10(11½)in. Instructions for larger sizes are in brackets.

Back
With 2½mm (No.12) needles cast on 85 (91) sts and work 10 rows K1, P1 rib. Change to 3mm (No.11) needles and cont in st st, comm with a K row. Work 66 (80) rows.
Shape raglan: Cast off 3 sts at beg of next 2 rows (79 (85) sts).*
Next row: K2 tog, K to end.
Next row: P2 tog, P to end.
Next row: K.
Next row: P.
Repeat the last 4 rows nine (eight) times more, 59 (67) sts.
Dec 1 st at beg of next and every following row until 43 sts rem.
Slip on to a stitch holder.

Front
As back to *.
Next row: K2 tog, K to end.
Next row: P2 tog, P to end.
Next row: K.
Next row: P.

Repeat the last 4 rows six (five) more times (65 (73) sts).
Dec 1 st at beg of next and every following row until 55 sts rem.
Shape neck: Left side: Next row: K2 tog, K9, slip rem sts (44) on to a stitch holder.
Dec 1 st at beg of next and every following row until 2 sts rem.
Cast off.
Right side: Hold centre 33 sts on stitch holder, rejoin yarn to rem 11 sts and K2 tog, K to end.
Dec 1 st at beg of next and every following row until 2 sts rem.
Cast off.

Right sleeve
With 2½mm (No.12) needles cast on 43 (47) sts and work 10 rows K1, P1 rib. Change to 3mm (No.11) needles and cont in st st, comm with a K row.
Inc 1 st at beg and end of next and every following 10th row until there are 59 (65) sts.
Cont without shaping until 96 (110) rows have been worked from comm, ending with a P row.
Shape raglan: Cast off 3 sts at beg of next 2 rows 53 (59) sts.
2-3 years size only: Next row: K2 tog, K to end.
Next row: P2 tog, P to end.
Next row: K.
Next row: P.
Repeat the last 4 rows two more times (47 sts).*
Both sizes: Dec 1 st at beg of next and every following row until 11 sts rem, ending with a P row.
Next row: Cast off 3 sts, K to end.
Dec 1 st at beg of next and every following row until 2 sts rem.
Cast off.

Left sleeve
As right sleeve to *.
Both sizes: Dec 1 st at beg of next and

every following row until 12 sts rem,
ending with a K row.
Next row: Cast off 3 sts, P to end.
Dec 1 st at beg of next and every follow-
ing row until 2 sts rem.
Cast off.

Neckband
Join raglan seams, leaving right side
back seam open.
With 2½mm (No.12) needle pick up 13
sts from right sleeve top, 47 sts from
front neck, 12 sts from left sleeve top
and 43 sts across back neck (115 sts).
Work 10 rows K1, P1 rib.
Cast off loosely in rib.

Make up
Follow pressing instructions on ball
band. Join raglan seam, leaving
neckband open. Join side and sleeve
seams. Work a buttonhole covered loop
on neckband edge and sew on button to
correspond.

Variations
Hand-knitted tee and sweat shirts are
very hard-wearing and if washed
correctly will outlast any cheap kind
bought in a shop. The ribbed hems will
prevent bagging. For small children,
paintbox bright colours look best.

17 Shirred top dress and skirt

The greatest effect for the least effort;
an oblong of fabric and a few rows of
elastic can make a dress, a skirt, a
nightie or a little something for a
twinkly ballerina.

90 cms (36 in)

50 (60) cms (20(24) in)

Fabric: *2-3 years:* 50cm (20in) of 90cm (36in) wide fabric – fine cotton or voile. *4-5 years:* 60cm (24in) of 90cm (36in) wide fabric.

Notions: Shirring elastic, 2m (2¼yd) of narrow ribbon, matching thread.

1 With right sides together sew a seam joining short sides of fabric to form a tube. Press. This seam is the centre back seam.
2 Neaten top edge by turning over a tiny hem and sewing down.
3 Starting 1.5cm (⅝in) away from top edge, machine five lines of shirring around the top in complete circuits of the fabric, starting and ending at the back seam. Space these rows the width of your sewing machine foot apart (see 'How To' guide, page 122).
4 Cut the ribbon into four lengths 50cm

(20in) long. Fit dress on child with seam at centre back. Position straps at front and back and slip stitch securely into place. Tie in bows on shoulder.
5 Turn up required hem. Press.

Variations
This is the easiest dress to make and its variations are endless. It will fit any child. To make the pattern simply measure from the child's underarm to the length of skirt required, plus 3cm (1¼in) for the hem. The width is always the same, 90cm (36in). Then follow instructions for making up. Here are some suggestions on variations:

1 A sun dress.
2 With tee shirts and blouses it makes a versatile pinafore dress.
3 A short nightie made in fine fabric.
4 A long nightie.
5 A ballet dress.
6 A skirt. This time measure from the waist to hem, and sew fewer lines of shirring elastic.

And for party dresses and skirts, pretty up by adding a nice deep frill at the hem.

18 Knit-and-quilt coat

The warmest, most versatile coat. Knit the lining and this makes the pattern for the quilted side – simply cut round and bind the two together.

For girls, make it in a pretty quilting with bows. For boys it looks good in camel-coloured wool with toggles. Line both with knitting.

It can be a jacket, a coat or a dressing gown.

A. KNITTED LINING

Yarn: Of chunky style yarn: 10 (13) 50g balls for jacket, 12 (15) 50g balls for coat.

Needles: A pair of 6mm (No.4).

Tension: 14 sts and 28 rows to 10cm (4in) square measured over g st on 6mm (No.4) needles.

Measurements: To fit ages 2-3 (4-5); actual chest measurement 70(75)cm, $27\frac{1}{2}(29\frac{1}{2})$in; jacket length 39(44)cm, $15\frac{1}{2}(17\frac{1}{2})$in; coat length 52(57)cm, $20\frac{1}{2}(22\frac{1}{2})$in; sleeve seam 25(30)cm, 10(12)in.
Instructions for larger sizes are in brackets.

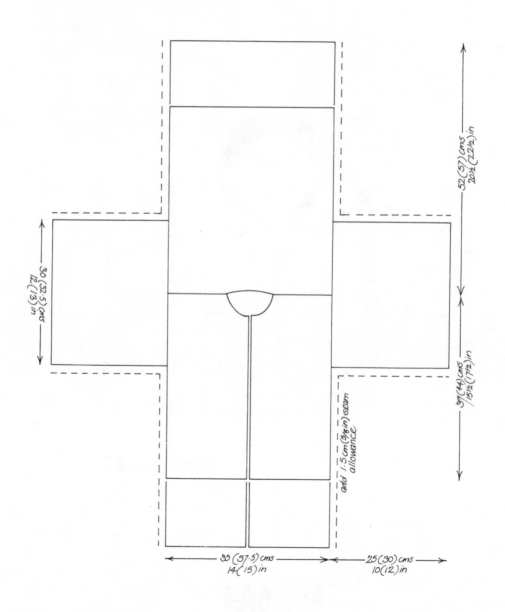

30 (32·5) cms
12 (13) in

52 (57) cms
20½ (22½) in

39 (44) cms
15½ (17½) in

add 1·5cm (⅝in) seam allowance

35 (37·5) cms
14 (15) in

25 (30) cms
10 (12) in

Back

Cast on 51 (55) sts and cont in g st.
Work 106 (120) rows for jacket, 142 (156) rows for coat.
Next row: K16 (17), slip rem sts (35, 38) on to a stitch holder.
Work 4 rows.
Cast off.
Cast off centre 19 (21) sts and work 4 rows on rem 16 (17) sts.
Cast off.

Left front

Cast on 25 (27) sts and cont in g st.
Work 93 (107) rows for jacket, 129 (143) rows for coat.
*Next row: Cast off 4 (5) sts, K to end.
Next row: K.
Next row: K2 tog, K to end.
Repeat the last two rows three more times (16 (17) sts).
Work 4 rows.
Cast off.

Right front

Cast off 25 (27) sts and cont in g st.
Work 92 (106) rows for jacket, 128 (142) rows for coat.
Cont as for left front from *.

Sleeves (2 alike)

Cast on 44 (48) sts and cont in g st.
Work 70 (84) rows.
Cast off.

Optional collar

Cast on 45 (49) sts and cont in g st.
Work 22 rows.
Cast off.

Make up

Follow pressing instructions on ball band. Join shoulder seams. Sew sleeves to body, folding in half and matching fold to shoulder seam.

If you want this lining to be worn on its own, sew the remaining seams.

B. QUILTED OUTER LAYER

Fabric: *Short jacket:* 1m (1⅛yd) of 90cm (36in) wide fabric. *Long jacket:* 1.20m (1⅜yd) of 90cm (36in) wide fabric.

Notions: 2 cards bias binding and matching thread.

1 With right sides together, take the knitted section and lay on top of the quilted fabric. Pin the layers together.
2 Cut all round, close to the knitted layer, making sure you add 1.5cm (⅝in) extra at side and underarm edges for seams. Take out pins.
3 With right sides together pin and sew underarm and side seams in one. Clip curves and press. Sew side and underarm seams of knitted layer also.
4 With *wrong* sides together slip knitted coat inside quilt coat and pin all round raw edges.
5 Make front ties: Take six (or four) pieces of bias binding, 30cm (12in) long. Fold in half lengthways and top stitch through. Pin and tack them in position on front edges.
6 Bind all round front and neck edges, plus hem, in one, starting and ending at a side seam.
7 Bind all round sleeve hems, starting and ending at underarm seam.

Collared coat

Cut out fabric, and sew both sets of side and underarm seams in usual way (see point 3 above).

1 Take collar and, with right sides together, sandwich between the two layers at neck edge. Sew in collar. Clip fabric allowance, turn out and press.
2 Continue as for first coat, but omit neck binding and front fastenings. Position and sew on toggles and cord fastenings.

Variations

There are endless permutations with this little coat. Here are just a few.

Jackets: One side knitted, reverse side quilted. Or one side knitted, reverse side in denim.

Coats: One side check quilting, reverse side knitted. Or one side tweedy knit, reverse side camel wool with wooden toggle buttons.

Why not make it as a dressing gown? For girls, make in the palest pink knit one side, and flower-sprigged quilting on the reverse. For boys, knit in navy for one side, with tartan quilting on the reverse.

9 Loose shirt and pyjamas

A loose-fitting shirt and blouse, with a small button-down collar for the boys, and a lace-trimmed, Peter Pan collar for the girls. Make the shirt and trousers (use pattern 11, page 43) in brushed cotton and you have lovely cosy pyjamas.

Sizes: Shown on layout thus:
2-3 years ——
4-5 years - - - - -

Fabric: 1.30m (1½yd) of 90cm (36in) wide cotton fabric.

Notions: *Boys:* 8 shirt buttons; *Girls:* 6 buttons, lace trimming, small piece of interfacing for collar, cut from chosen collar pattern.

1 With right sides together place the two pieces of the collar you have chosen together, and place collar piece cut from interfacing on top. Sew through all three thicknesses all round collar omitting neck edge.
2 Trim interfacing right up to stitching line. Trim rest of seam allowance, clip edges, turn through and press. Attach lace to underside of collar at this stage.
3 With right sides together place two front pieces on back piece and sew shoulder seams. Either press open or

fell this seam (see 'How To' guide, page 122).

4 Take collar and, with right sides together, pin collar to neckline matching centre back of collar to centre back of blouse. Collar ends 3cm (1¼in) away from front edge.

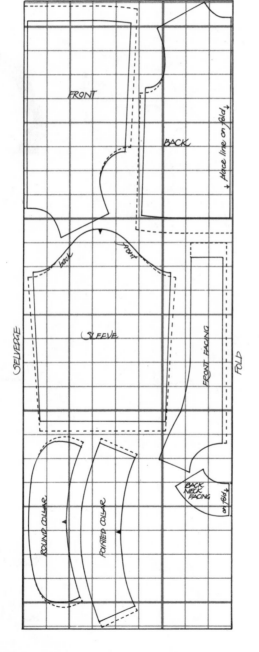

5 With right sides together sew back neck facing to front neck facing across shoulder seams. Press open. Neaten raw outside edge.

6 With right sides together pin complete facing to blouse fronts and across neck, sandwiching the collar between the facing and the blouse. Sew all round, clip corners, turn through to inside of blouse and press. Catch each facing to each shoulder seam with a slip stitch.

7 Mark first buttonhole (left side for boys, right for girls), the centre of the top buttonhole to be 1.5cm (⅝in) down from neck seam and 2cm (¾in) in from front edge. Evenly position 5 more buttonholes down front, and work. Match buttons on other front and sew on.

8 Open blouse out and lay flat.

9 Run a line of gathering around head of sleeve.

10 With right sides together, and matching tops of sleeves with shoulder seam and armhole edges, pin in sleeves, easing by pulling up gathering thread. Sew in, clip curves and press.

11 Sew sleeve underarm and side seam in one, with right sides together and taking care to match armhole seams. Clip and press. Sew in second sleeve in same way.

12 Neaten sleeve hems, then turn up and press a 1.5cm (⅝in) hem on each. Sew leaving a gap in each to insert elastic. Run elastic through, adjust to fit and secure ends.

13 The hem: Open out front facings and neaten lower edge all round by turning over a tiny hem. Then fold facings to front of the blouse so that right sides are together. Machine a 2cm (¾in) seam across the bottom of the facing at left front. Continue machining round hem and across bottom of right front facing which is

also turned back, right sides together.

Clip corners and turn facings out (this forms a neat faced corner). Press, and use the machine line around the bottom as a guide to turning up a 2cm ($\frac{3}{4}$in) hem. Press and hem by hand.

Variations

This pattern is for a basic shirt, but one you can use in lots of ways. Here are a few suggestions:

For girls:
1 Trim the collar and sleeve hems with lace.
2 Sew on pretty matching ribbon bows at the neck.

For boys:
1 Make in checked cotton, with a yoke shape defined by a fringed braid.
2 Make in denim with slogan patches.

20 Rain suit

A glistening Ciré rain suit, with a big roomy hood and a nice chunky zip that's easy for little fingers to manage. It has elasticated wrists – no rain up the sleeves – and elasticated ankles – no water in the wellies.

Why not make it in knit fabric for a terrific track suit?

Sizes: Shown on layout thus:
2-3 years ———
4-5 years - - - - -

Fabric: *Jacket:* 1.50m (1⅝yd) of 90cm (36in) wide showerproof fabric.
Trousers: 1.25m (1⅜yd) of 90cm (36in) wide showerproof fabric.

Notions: 32 or 36cm (13 or 14in) open-ended zip, cord for hood and hem, elastic for trouser waistband, narrow elastic and matching thread.

Before you start: The cutting and sewing instructions for the rain suit trousers are the same as for the harem trousers, pattern No.11, on page 43. But when cutting the pattern add 1.5cm (⅝in) down side seams on back and front pattern pieces. This will make the rain trousers nice and roomy.

1 Mark and work the two buttonholes in the hood pieces, marked E for 2-3 years, and F for 4-5 years.

74

front facing. Fold facing back and tack down, sandwiching hood between jacket and facing. Sew right round neck edge. Take out tacking,

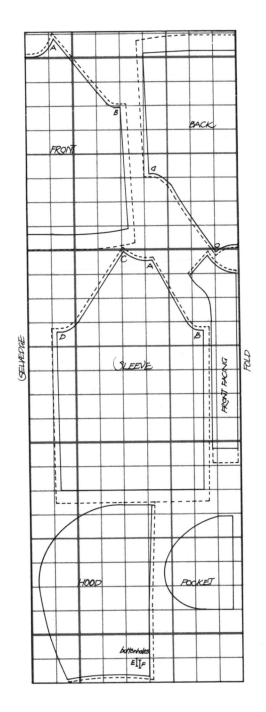

2 With right sides together sew curving back seam on hood. Fell this seam (see 'How To' guide, page 122).

3 Neaten front edge of hood by turning over a tiny hem and pressing. Then turn back and sew a 1.5cm ($\frac{5}{8}$in) hem round front edge.

4 With right sides together match moints A and B on jacket front and sleeve front, sew between these two points. Clip curves and press. Repeat on second front.

5 With right sides together match points C and D on jacket back and sleeve back, sew between these two points. Clip curves and press. Repeat on second sleeve and back.

6 Take front facing and neaten shoulder edge. With right sides together pin front facing to jacket front and sew. Repeat on other front edge.

7 With right sides together pin bottom of hood to neck edge matching centre back of hood to centre back of jacket and match hood edges to seam of

clip corners, turn out facing and press.

8 Slip stitch neatened shoulder edge of facing to front raglan seam.

9 Press hood seam towards jacket, stitch seam allowance down 3mm ($\frac{1}{8}$in) below first stitch line, through all thicknesses. Trim raw edges close to stitching.

10 With right sides together and taking care to match armhole seams, sew underarm and side seam in one. Clip curves and trim. Press.

11 Neaten sleeve hem then turn up a 1.5cm ($\frac{5}{8}$in) hem and stitch down leaving a gap to insert elastic. Thread elastic through hem, adjust to fit and secure.

12 Open zip. Place zip sections, right side up, under front edges and with the top close to neck seam, having turned under taped edges of zip at top, tack and sew into place. Check that zip runs smoothly and that top and bottom match.

13 Neaten bottom edge of jacket, then turn up hem and sew down. Press. Slot cord through buttonholes and channel round hood, knot ends and tie. Thread cord through hem, knot ends and tie.

Variations
Lots of mileage out of this little suit.

1 In Ciré, it's a practical rain suit.
2 In knitted fabric, it's a track suit.
3 And in just about any fabric you like it's a zippy jacket.

21 Bobble hats and scarves

Super snug hats and scarves – knit them in lots of colours to match all their coats and jackets.

For girls, the bobbles made in red and black look like perky little ladybirds.

For boys, knit them in their favourite team's colours. Make the bobbles in black and white just like mini footballs.

figure 1

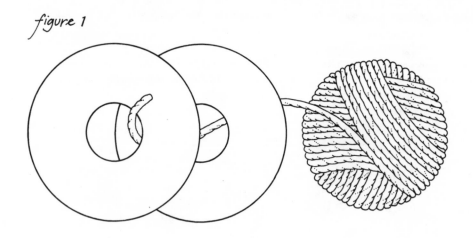

figure 2 ~ LADYBIRD

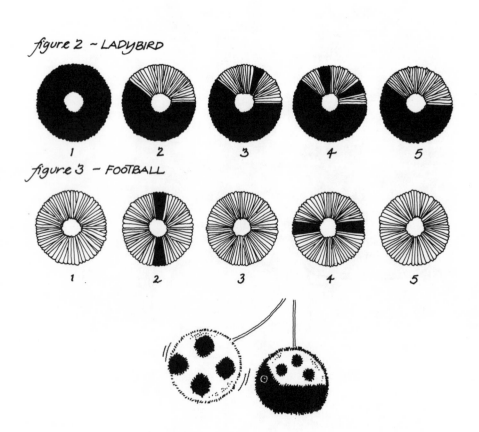

1   2   3   4   5

figure 3 ~ FOOTBALL

1   2   3   4   5

Yarn: Two 50g balls double knitting yarn. *Ladybird hat and scarf:* 2 balls red double knitting yarn, plus a small quantity of black. *Football hat and scarf:* 1 ball each of team's colours, plus small amount of black and white.

Needles: A pair of 3½mm (No.9).

Tension: 20 sts and 32 rows worked over 10cm (4in) or rib, slightly stretched.

Hat

With 3½mm (No.9) needles, cast on 100 sts and cont in K2, P2 rib.
Work 80 rows.

Next row: K2 tog to end (50 sts). Break yarn, thread through stitches, draw up and fix. Join seam.
Sew on bobble (see below) and turn back cuff.

Scarf

With 3½mm (No.9) needles, cast on 36 sts and cont in K2, P2 rib.
Work 360 rows (for football scarf, work stripes of 40 rows each.)
Cast off.
Gather up both ends of scarf and attach bobbles (see below).

Bobbles

Yarn: Small amount of double knitting wool in two contrasting colours.
Some stiff card.

1 Cut two 10cm (4in) circles of card with a 2.5cm (1in) hole in the centre. (Figure 1.)
2 Place rings together and wind wool in rounds to cover card completely.
3 *For ladybird (Figure 2.)*
Round one: in black only.
Rounds two to five: in red and black, as diagrams.
4 *For football (Figure 3.)*
Rounds one, three and five: in white only.

Rounds two and four: white and black, as diagram.

5 Push scissor points through wool at outside edge and between two layers of card and cut all round.
6 Take a length of yarn, slide between the two layers of card and tie round tightly.
7 Slide off card rings and trim bobble with scissors to form an even ball.
8 Attach to hat and scarf using remainder of tying yarn.

Monogram jackets (page 52).

Six to Eleven Years

Pyjamas (page 71), kimono dressing gown (page 97), and shirred-top nightie (page 64).

22 Girls' dungarees and sun dress

Two essentials for a happy summer holiday. Painter's overalls, with a comfortable elasticated waistline and knotted straps. Or a pretty sundress in the same style. Easy to make, easy to wear.

Sizes: Shown on layout thus:
6-7 years ——
8-9 years - - - - -
10-11 years -·-·-·-

Fabric: *6-7 years:* 2.10m (2¼yd) of 90cm (36in) wide fabric. *8-9 years:* 2.20m (2⅜yd) of 90cm (36in) wide fabric. *10-11 years:* 2.30m (2½yd) of 90cm (36in) wide fabric.

Notions: A piece of iron-on interfacing cut the same size as one bodice band, matching thread, shirring elastic.

1 Mark shirring lines, with chalk or tacking, on front and back trouser sections.
2 Take the two bodice bands. On the wrong side of one band iron on the interfacing. With right sides together sew round two short and one long side of band. Clip corners, trim seam allowance, turn through and press.
3 With right sides together place the two front trouser sections together

*Note: This diagram has been divided
into two parts. Do not cut your fabric in
two – the layout should be continuous.*

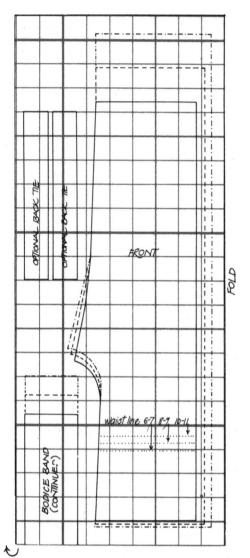

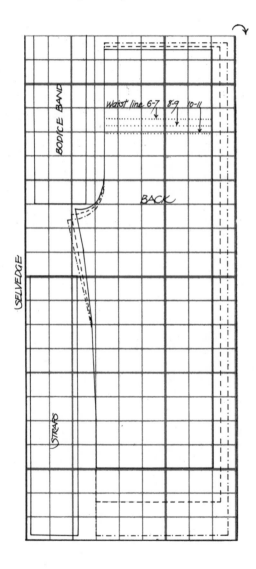

and sew the curving centre front
seam. Clip curve and press.

4 Repeat with curving back seam, but
leave an opening of 10cm (4in) at top
edge. Clip curves and press. Press
back 1.5cm ($\frac{5}{8}$in) turnings at openings and top stitch down. With right
sides together, sew side seams and
press.

5 Run two or three lines of shirring
round the marked line, starting and
ending at the centre back seam (see
'How To' guide, page 122).

6 With right sides together and taking care to match centre front and back seams, sew the inside leg seams in one, from trouser hem to trouser hem.

7 Run two lines of machine stitching around the top edge of the trousers and gently gather up until it exactly matches the length of the stiffened bodice band.

8 With right sides together, pin stiffened side of bodice band to dungaree top. Evenly distribute gathers, pin and sew.

9 Press seam allowance towards band. Turn a 1.5cm ($\frac{5}{8}$in) hem up along the inside raw edge of band, press and slip stitch to inside of dungarees along previous stitching line. Press band.

10 Neaten trouser hems by turning up a tiny hem. Turn up a 1.5cm ($\frac{5}{8}$in) hem, leaving a small gap to insert elastic.

11 Run elastic through hem, adjust to fit and secure.

12 Take one shoulder strap, fold in half lengthways, sew one long and one short side, trim seam allowance and turn through. Press. Turn short end in 1.5cm ($\frac{5}{8}$in) and tack across. Top stitch all round strap. Take out tacking and press. Repeat with second strap.

13 Sew two tiny hooks and eyes on each side of the bodice band at top and bottom close to the edge. Try on the dungarees and position the straps on each side of the centre back opening; pin. Put straps over the shoulders and mark position of buttonholes on front band.

14 Work buttonholes. Top stitch straps on to back band in a cross pattern. Slot straps through buttonholes and tie knots.

Variations

Make the sun dress version as follows:

1 Cut bodice and straps as dungaree pattern.

2 Take a piece of fabric 90cm (36in) wide by the length of dress required, plus 3cm (1$\frac{1}{4}$in) for a hem.

3 With right sides together sew centre back seam down short edges making a tube and leaving a 10cm (4in) gap at top edge. Press seam. Press seam allowance back at opening and top stitch round.

4 Attach to band as for dungarees.

5 Turn up hem.

84

23 Boys' and girls' ski sweater, hat and mitts

Sporty ski-style sweater – snowflakes
give it a wintry look, bright colours
warm it up.
   Plus a pull-on bobble hat and cosy
mitts.

Yarn: Of Aran style yarn: *Sweater:* 4
(5,6) 50g balls MC, 1 (1,2) 50g balls LC,
2 (2,3) 50g balls DC. *Hat and Mitts:* 2
50g balls LC, 2 50g balls DC and an odd-
ment of MC.

Needles: A pair each of 3¼mm (No.10)
and 4mm (No.8).

Tension: 19 sts and 26 rows to 10cm
(4in) square, measured over st st on
4mm (No.8) needles.

Measurements: To fit ages 6-7 (8-9, 10-
11): actual chest measurement 76(81,86)
cm, 30(32,34)in; length 44(49,53)cm,
17½(19,21)in; sleeve seam 33(37,40)cm,
13(14½,16)in.
Instructions for larger sizes are in
brackets.

Back
With 3¼mm (No.10) needles and DC
cast on 73 (77, 81) sts and work 14 rows
K1, P1 rib.
Change to 4mm (No.8) needles and MC

and cont in st st, comm with a K row.
Work 44 (54, 64) rows.
Change to LC and DC and work heart
motif (14 rows) from pattern (shaded sts
in DC), reading K rows from right to left
and P rows from left to right, and starting at correct point for the size required.
Change to MC and LC and work 22 rows
of snowflake motif in same manner
(shaded sts in MC).*

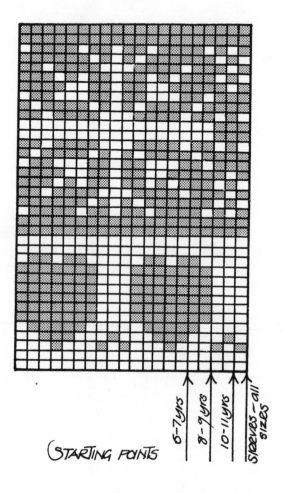

(STARTING POINTS

6-7 yrs
8-7 yrs
10-11 yrs
sleeves - all sizes

Change to DC and work 20 (22, 24) rows.
Shape shoulders: Cast off 7 (8, 8) sts at
beg of next 4 rows.
Cast off 7 (7, 9) sts at beg of next 2 rows.
Slip rem sts [31 (31, 31)] on to a stitch
holder.

Front
As back to *.
Change to DC and work 2 (4, 6) rows.
Divide for neck: Left side: Next row:
K26 (28, 30), slip rem sts (47, 49, 51) on
to a stitch holder.
Next row: P.
Next row: K.
Next row: P2 tog, P to end.
Repeat the last 2 rows four more times
(21 (23, 25) sts).
Work a further 6 rows without shaping.
Shape shoulder: Next row: Cast off 7 (8,
8) sts, K to end.
Next row: P.
Repeat the last 2 rows once more.
Cast off rem 7 (7, 9) sts.
Right side: Hold centre 21 sts on stitch
holder, rejoin yarn to rem 26 (28, 30) sts
and K to end.
Next row: P.
Next row: K2 tog, K to end.
Repeat the last 2 rows four more times
(21 (23, 25) sts).
Work a further 8 rows without shaping.
Shape shoulder: Next row: Cast off 7 (8,
8) sts, P to end.
Next row: K.
Repeat the last 2 rows once more.
Cast off rem 7 (7, 9) sts.

Sleeves (2 alike)
With 3¼mm (No.10) needles and DC
cast on 37 (39, 41) sts and work 14 rows
K1, P1 rib.
Change to 4mm (No.8) needles and MC
and cont in st st, comm with a K row.
Inc 1 st at beg and end of next and every
following 4th (4th, 6th) row until there
are 63 (65, 67) sts on the needle.
Cont without shaping until 70 (80, 90)
rows have been worked from comm ending with a P row.
Change to LC and DC and work heart
motif (14 rows), starting at point
indicated for sleeve.
Cast off.

Neckband

Join left shoulder seams. With 3¼mm (No.10) needle pick up 17 sts down right side of neck, 21 sts from centre, 16 sts up left side of neck, and 31 sts across back neck (85 sts).
With DC work 8 rows K1, P1 rib.
Cast off loosely in rib.

Make up

Follow pressing instructions on ball band. Join right shoulder and neckband seams. Join side seams up to top of heart motif. Join sleeve seams. Sew sleeves into armholes.

Hat

With 3¼mm (No.10) needles and LC cast on 95 sts and work 26 rows K1, P1 rib, inc 1 st at end of last row (96 sts).
Change to 4mm (No.8) needles and DC and cont in st st, comm with a K row.
Work 20 rows.
Shape crown: Next row: *Sl 1, K1, PSSO, K12, K2 tog* repeat from * to * to end.
Next and every following alt row: P.
Next row: *Sl 1, K1, PSSO, K10, K2 tog* repeat from * to * to end.
Cont in this manner dec K sts by 2 each time, until the following row has been worked: *Sl 1, K1, PSSO, K2 tog* repeat from * to * end (12 sts).
Break yarn, thread through sts on needle, draw up and fix.
Join seam.
Make bobble or tassel in MC and attach to crown.

Mitts (2 alike)

With 3¼mm (No.10) needles and LC cast on 39 sts and work 20 rows K1, P1 rib.
Change to 4mm (No.8) needles and DC and cont in st st, comm with a K row.
Work 14 rows.
Next row: K14, Sl next 11 sts for thumb on to a safety pin, K rem 14 sts (28 sts).

Work 11 rows ending with a P row.
1st row: *Sl 1, K1, PSSO, K10, K2 tog* repeat from * to * once more.
2nd, 4th, 6th and 8th rows: P.
3rd row: *Sl 1, K1, PSSO, K8, K2 tog* repeat from * to * once more.
5th row: *Sl 1, K1, PSSO, K6, K2 tog* repeat from * to * once more.
7th row: *Sl 1, K1, PSSO, K4, K2 tog* repeat from * to * once more.
Cast off.
Thumb: Pick up the 11 sts from safety pin, rejoin yarn, and work 14 rows. Break yarn, thread through sts on needle, draw up and fix. Join thumb seam. Join side seam of mitt.

Variations

Go on! Try this pattern – it really is a smashing sweater! But you feel unsure about fair-isle knitting? Try knitting a trial sample. Still not happy? – well, leave out the motifs and simply knit bold stripes.

24 Boys' and girls' shirt

Super smart shirts with small, neat collars, back yokes and nice curvy hems to tuck in or leave out as they wish.

Sizes: Shown on layout thus:
6-7 years ——
8-9 years - - - - -
10-11 years - - - - - -

Fabric: 2.10m (2⅜yd) of 90cm (36in) wide shirt fabric.

Notions: 8 shirt buttons, iron-on interfacing for cuffs and front facing, non iron-on interfacing for collar, matching thread.

Before you start: Measure from neck to hem along front fold where indicated on pattern and cut two strips of iron-on interfacing the same length by 4cm (1½in) wide, to stiffen front edges. Cut two pieces of iron-on interfacing 22 × 5.5cm (8½ × 2in) to stiffen cuffs. Cut required collar shape in non iron-on interfacing.

1 Take front section and mark front fold. Iron interfacing on to wrong side of facing up to fold edge. Turn over and stitch a tiny hem all down facing

edge. Repeat with second front.

2 Fold facing to inside of shirt and press fold line. Tack shoulder edge of facing to shoulder edge of shirt. Repeat on second front.

3 Take one yoke piece and lay flat, with right side uppermost. Then take the two front pieces and, with right sides uppermost, match the shoulder lines and tack.

Note: This diagram has been divided into two parts, but there is no need to divide your fabric. Just continue from the first layout to the second.

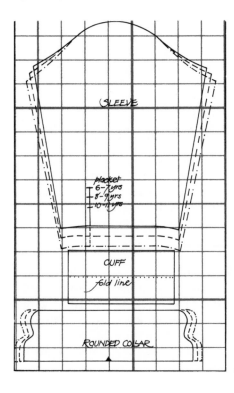

FRONT

fold line

SLEEVE

placket
6-7 yrs
8-9 yrs
10-11 yrs

CUFF

fold line

ROUNDED COLLAR

FOLD

place lines on fold

BACK

POINTED COLLAR

SELVEDGE

YOKE

4 Take second yoke piece and, with wrong side uppermost, pin across shoulders on top of first yoke. Sew through three layers on both shoulders, trim seams and press yoke away from shirt front.

5 Turn under a 1.5cm (⅝in) hem along bottom of yoke on inside of shirt and tack.

6 With right sides together sew shirt back to remaining raw edge of yoke. Press seam allowance towards yoke.

7 Turn to inside. Match tacked edge of yoke to previous stitch line. Pin and top stitch down.

8 Run a line of gathering around both sleeve heads. Lay shirt out flat with right side uppermost. Matching one sleeve top with shoulder seam and matching armhole edges, pin and ease in by drawing up gathering line. Sew in and press seam. Repeat with second sleeve.

9 Place collar pieces with right sides together and lay collar interfacing on top. Sew all round through three thicknesses, leaving bottom edge free. Trim seam allowance and clip curves. Turn out and press.

10 Pin one layer of collar plus interfacing to neck edge of shirt, matching centre back of shirt to centre back of collar and matching ends of collar to front edges of shirt. Sew, press seam towards collar, clip and trim.

11 Fold under a 1.5cm (⅝in) hem on inside raw edge of collar, press and match to previous sewing line, then top stitch down. Top stitch outside edge of collar.

12 Cut two facings for sleeve openings from shirt fabric 12 × 5cm (5 × 2in). Cut a slit 8cm (3in) long up the centre of the facing, starting at one short edge. (Neaten all round, except for cut edge.)

13 With right sides together place facing for sleeve opening on to sleeve opening and stitch round the slit, very close to the edge. Turn through to inside of sleeve and press and top stitch round opening.

14 With right sides together, and taking care to match armhole seams, sew underarm and side seam in one, press and fell this seam (see 'How To' guide, page 122). Repeat. with second side.

15 Take cuff and iron interfacing on to wrong side. Repeat with second cuff. With right sides together fold cuff lengthways and sew each short side. Repeat with second cuff. Clip corners, turn out and press.

16 Run a line of gathering around sleeve hems close to edge.

17 With right sides together pin one cuff layer with interfacing to sleeve hem. Draw up gathering to fit. Sew and press seam towards cuff. (If you prefer, put 2 small pleats at sleeve hem instead of gathering.)

18 Turn a 1.5cm (⅝in) hem under on remaining edge of cuff and press. Match edge to previous line of stitching, pin and top stitch down.

19 Turn up a 6mm (¼in) hem all round bottom of shirt and tack, then turn up the same amount again. Sew and press.

20 Mark buttonhole on centre front of neck band (right for girls, left for boys). Mark next buttonhole 2cm (¾in) down. Space 5 more buttonholes evenly down front. Work buttonholes, mark buttons on opposite front and sew on.

Variations

This shirt has all the grown-up details and it's lovely just as it is. But try ringing the changes with unusual fabrics. Shirts may be a little difficult at first, but do persevere; they get easier with practice.

25 Slim-fit trousers and shorts

Narrow-bottom trousers have a smooth-fitting, plain front, with patch pockets at the back. Make the short version for summer holidays and try fraying the hems to look like cut-offs.

Sizes: Shown on layout thus:
6-7 years ——
8-9 years - - - - -
10-11 years -·-·-·-·

Fabric: 1.20m (1⅜yd) of 115cm (45in) wide fabric, small piece of strong lining fabric and of iron-on interfacing for fly, and a strip of iron-on interfacing cut the same size as one waistband piece.

Notions: 15cm (6in) zip, one button or a bar-tack fastening.

Before you start: Be sure to cut 4 fly sections (2 in the trouser fabric and 2 in lining); you will only use three – it depends upon which trouser you make (boys' or girls') which of the 2 lining pieces you use. Read the instructions very carefully.

1 Take front section (right side for boys, left for girls) and lay flat with right side uppermost. Place zip with wrong side uppermost against centre front edge. Top stitch zip into place 5mm (¼in) in from edge.

2 Take one fly piece and iron interfacing on to wrong side. Neaten the outside curved edge. With right sides together, place interfaced fly section on to second trouser front, matching centre front seams. Sew into place. Trim away interfaced seam allowance. Fold back and press.

3 Take the two front trouser sections and, with right sides together, stitch curved crutch seam up to zip. Clip and press.

4 Pin and tack the fold edge of fly (left for boys, right for girls) to the opposite centre front edge, concealing the zip.

5 Turn to wrong side. Pin remaining free edge of zip to interfaced fly (take care not to pin through trouser layer). Sew zip in 5mm ($\frac{1}{4}$in) from edge of zip.

6 Turn back to right side. With tailors' chalk, or a tacking line, mark a line parallel to centre front (left side for boys, right for girls) and 3cm (1$\frac{1}{4}$in) away from it, curving base to a point 1.5cm ($\frac{5}{8}$in) below bottom of zip. Top stitch through both layers along line.

7 Take remaining main fly piece and appropriate fly piece in lining fabric and, with right sides together, sew outer curved edge. Clip, turn out and press. Top stitch 6mm ($\frac{1}{4}$in) in from outside curved edge.

8 Turn to wrong side, take finished fly section. Place raw edge of the fly 5mm ($\frac{1}{4}$in) past zip edge (thus concealing zip). Sew through all layers.

9 Take pocket piece and mark fold. Fold flap with right sides together and sew a 1.5cm ($\frac{5}{8}$in) seam down each side of flap. Clip corners, turn out and press. Fold under a 1.5cm ($\frac{5}{8}$in) turning all round rest of pocket and tack. Repeat with second pocket.

10 Top stitch pockets with a cross pattern, or as desired.

11 Position the pockets on both back trouser sections 2cm ($\frac{3}{4}$in) down from and level with the waist edge. Pin down and top stitch closely round three sides.

12 With right sides together, sew both side seams and press. Top stitch or fell this seam for a 'jeans' look (see 'How To' guide, page 122).

13 With right sides together match back trouser sections and sew centre back seam. Clip and press.

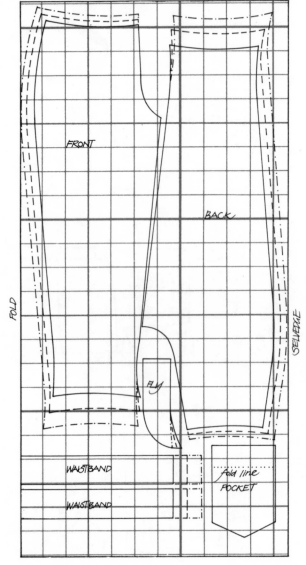

FRONT

BACK

FOLD

SELVEDGE

FLY

WAISTBAND

WAISTBAND

Fold line
POCKET

14 With right sides together, and taking care to match front and back seams, sew the inside leg seams in one. Clip and press.

15 Iron strip of interfacing to wrong side of one waistband section. With right sides together match waistband sections and sew both short and one long edge. Clip corners, turn out and press.

16 With right sides together, pin interfaced edge of waistband to trousers, matching ends of waistband to centre front edges of the trousers exactly. Sew and press seam towards the waistband. Clip seam and trim interfaced seam allowance.

17 Turn under a 1.5cm ($\frac{5}{8}$in) hem all along remaining raw edge of waistband and press. Match to previous stitching line and top stitch or slip stitch down on the inside of trousers.

18 Mark a buttonhole at centre front of waistband and work. Mark for button and sew on. Or stitch on a bar-tack and hook fastening.

19 Turn up hems as required.

Variations

These trousers are cut close. Use plenty of top stitching on all the seams and pockets for a jeans look.

The shorts are great for the beach; why not team them with a shirt in tropical print fabric?

26 Chunky-knit jacket

Quick-to-knit jacket – make it in unusual marled wool, with nice wooden toggle buttons and patch pockets.

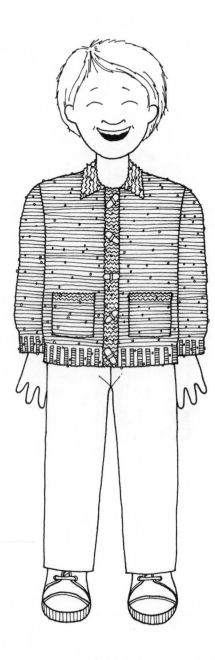

Yarn: Of chunky tweed style yarn: 8 (9, 10) 50g balls, plus 5 toggle buttons.

Needles: A pair each of 5½mm (No.5) and 6mm (No.4).

Tension: 15 sts and 20 rows to 10cm (4in) square measured over st st on 6mm (No.4) needles.

Measurements: To fit ages 6-7 (8-9, 10-11): actual chest measurement 76(81,86) cm, 30(32,34)in; length 44(49,53)cm, 17(19,21)in; sleeve seam 33(37,40)cm, 13 (14½,16)in.
Instructions for larger sizes are in brackets.

Back
With 5½mm (No.5) needles cast on 57 (61, 63) sts and work 10 rows K1, P1 rib.
Change to 6mm (No.4) needles and cont in st st, comm with a K row.
Work 46 (52, 60) rows.
Shape armholes: Cast off 4 sts at beg of next 2 rows (49 (53, 55) sts).

Next row: K.
Next row: P2 tog, P to end.
Repeat the last 2 rows four more times (9 (10, 11) sts).
Work 4 rows without shaping.
Shape shoulder: Next row: Cast off 5 sts, K to end.
Next row: P.
Cast off rem 4 (5, 6) sts.

Right front

With 5½mm (No.5) needles cast on 25 (27, 29) sts and work 10 rows K1, P1 rib.
Change to 6mm (No.4) needles and cont in st st, comm with a K row.
Work 47 (53, 61) rows.
Shape armhole: Cast off 4 sts, P to end (21 (23, 25) sts).
Next row: K.
Next row: P2 tog, P to end.
Repeat the last 2 rows until 18 (19, 20) sts rem.
Cont without shaping until 72 (80, 90) rows have been worked from comm, ending with a P row.
Shape neck: Cast off 4 sts, K to end.
Next row: P.
Next row: K2 tog, K to end.
Repeat last 2 rows four more times (9 (10, 11) sts).
Work 4 rows without shaping.
Shape shoulder: Next row: Cast off 5 sts, P to end.
Next row: K.
Cast off rem 4 (5, 6) sts.

Sleeves (2 alike)

With 5½mm (No.5) needles cast on 31 (33, 35) sts and work 10 rows K1, P1 rib.
Change to 6mm (No.4) needles and cont in st st, comm with a K row.
Inc 1 st at beg and end of next and every following 10th row until there are 41 (45, 49) sts on the needle.
Cont without shaping until 66 (72, 80) rows have been worked from comm.
Shape sleeve head: Cast off 4 sts at beg of next 2 rows (33 (37, 41) sts).

Dec 1 st at beg of next and every following row until 43 (45, 47) sts rem.
Cont without shaping until 88 (96, 106) rows have been worked from comm.
Shape shoulders: Cast off 5 sts at beg of next 2 rows.
Cast off 4 (5, 6) sts at beg of next 2 rows.
Cast off rem 25 sts.

Left front

With 5½mm (No.5) needles cast on 25 (27, 29) sts and work 10 rows K1, P1 rib.
Change to 6mm (No.4) needles and cont in st st, comm with a K row.
Work 46 (52, 60) rows.
Shape armhole: Next row: Cast off 4 sts, K to end (21 (23, 25) sts).
Next row: P.
Next row: K2 tog, K to end.
Repeat the last 2 rows until 18 (19, 20) sts rem.
Cont without shaping until 73 (81, 91) rows have been worked from comm, ending with a K row.
Shape neck: Cast off 4 sts, P to end.

6-7 and 8-9 year sizes only: Next row: K2 tog, K to end.
Next row: P2 tog, P to end.
Next row: K.
Next row: P.
6-7 year sizes only: Repeat the last 4 rows once more.
All sizes: Dec 1 st at beg of next and every following row until 15 sts rem. Cast off.

Button band
With 5½mm (No.5) needles cast on 8 sts and cont in g st.
Work 102 (114, 128) rows.
Cast off.

Buttonhole band
With 5½mm (No.5) needles cast on 8 sts and cont in g st.
Work 6 (4, 4) rows.
1st row: K3, cast off 2 sts, K3.
2nd row: K3, cast on 2 sts, K3.
Work 20 (24, 28) rows.
Repeat the last 22 (26, 30) rows three more times, then 1st and 2nd rows once more (5 buttonholes).
Work 6 (4, 4) rows.
Cast off.

Pockets (2 pieces alike)
With 6mm (No.4) needles cast on 14 sts and cont in st st, comm with a K row.
Work 16 rows.
Work 6 rows g st.
Cast off.

Collar
Join shoulder seams. With 6mm (No.4) needle pick up 17 sts from left neck, 25 sts from back neck, and 17 sts from right neck (59 sts).
Work 20 rows g st.
Cast off.

Make up
Follow pressing instructions on ball band. Join side seams and sleeve seams.

Sew sleeves into armholes. Sew button and buttonhole bands to fronts. Position and sew on toggles. Position and sew on pockets.

Variations
The tweedy yarn really perks up this simple jacket. For a real Technicolour Dream Coat, knit the jacket in bold multi-coloured stripes.

Ski sweater (page 85), pinafore skirt (page 103), and girls' shirt (page 88).

7 Kimono dressing gown

Stylish kimonos – the easiest kind of
dressing gown to make. And they look
smashing too! Make it plain or
embroider it for a touch of the exotic.

*Chunky-knit jackets (page 94), and
slim-fit trousers (page 91).*

Sizes: Shown on layout thus:
6-7 years ——
8-9 years - - - - -
10-11 years -··—··—

Fabric: *6-7 years:* 1.95m (2⅛yd) of 115cm (45in) wide fabric. *8-9 years:* 2.10m (2⅜yd) of 115cm (45in) wide fabric. *10-11 years:* 2.20m (2½yd) of 115cm (45in) wide fabric.

Notions: Matching thread.

1 Pocket: Take pocket piece and mark fold. Fold over flap and with right sides together stitch a 1.5cm (⅝in) seam at each side of flap. Clip corners turn out and press. Press a 1.5cm (⅝in) hem all round rest of pocket. Pin pocket in place (left side for boys, right for girls) and top stitch down.

2 Take two back pieces and, with right sides together, sew back seam. Press or fell (see 'How To' guide, page 122).

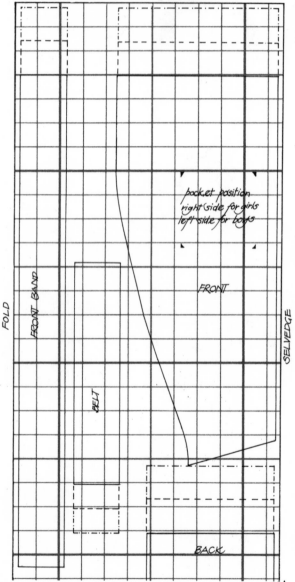

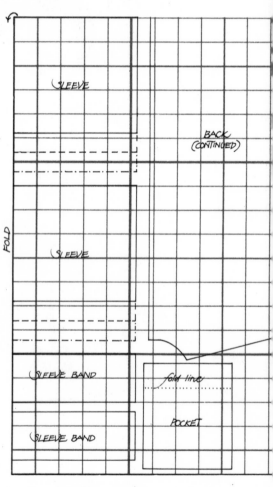

Note: This diagram has been divided into two parts. Do not cut your fabric in two – the layout should be continuous, as shown by the arrows.

3 With right sides together place two front sections on back section and sew shoulder seams. Press or fell.

4 Open out dressing gown flat with right side uppermost. With right sides together match centre of sleeve top with shoulder seam and sew sleeve in flat. Repeat with second sleeve. Press or fell.

5 With right sides together, and taking care to match armhole seams, sew underarm and side seam in one. Press or fell.

6 Take the two front band sections and, with right sides together, sew together at one short edge. Press open. Fold over and press a 1.5cm ($\frac{5}{8}$in) hem along one long edge.

7 With right sides together, and matching centre back seam of band to centre back seam of dressing gown, pin and sew the long raw edge of band up left front, across neck and down right front. Press seam allowance towards band.

8 Neaten bottom edge, then fold up and sew a 2.5cm (1in) hem all round dressing gown. Do not sew across bottom of front bands – simply press them up.

9 Fold front band to inside, matching edge to sewing line. Tack, press and top stitch band down. Press, fold edge, remove tacking.

10 Take two belt sections and, with right sides together, sew short ends together. Press open. Fold belt in half lengthways, sew all round raw edges, leaving a small gap in the centre of long edge. Trim seam allowance, turn out and press. Slip stitch the opening.

11 Take sleeve band and, with right sides together, sew across short edge to form a circle. Press seam open. Press up a 1.5cm ($\frac{5}{8}$in) hem all round one edge and attach the other edge, with right sides together, to the sleeve hem (matching underarm seams). Press seam allowance towards band. Repeat with second sleeve band.

12 Fold band to inside, matching edge to previous stitching line. Top stitch down. Repeat with second sleeve band.

Variations

These look great in their very simplest form – but why not:

For boys: tuck piping under front and sleeve bands?
For girls: tuck broderie anglaise under front bands? Or, how about doing it properly and embroidering a huge motif on the back?

28 Vee~neck pyjamas and nightie

No fuss pyjamas; a pull-on tee-shirt shaped top, with bermudas – to make a nice change.

The nightie is just a longer version of the pyjama top.

Sizes: Shown on layout thus:
6-7 years ——
8-9 years - - - - -
10-11 years -·-··-··-

Fabric: *Pyjamas:* 1.50m (1¾yd) of 150cm (60in) wide fabric. *Nightie:* 1.20m (1⅜yd) of 150cm (60in) wide fabric.

Notions: Matching thread, waistband elastic.

Pyjama top

1 With right sides together, place two back sections together and sew down centre back. Press.
2 With right sides together place back and front sections together and sew across shoulder seams. Press.
3 Take back and front neck facings and, with right sides together, sew across shoulder seams. Press seams open. Fold under, press and tack a 1.5cm (⅝in) turning all round outside edge of facing.

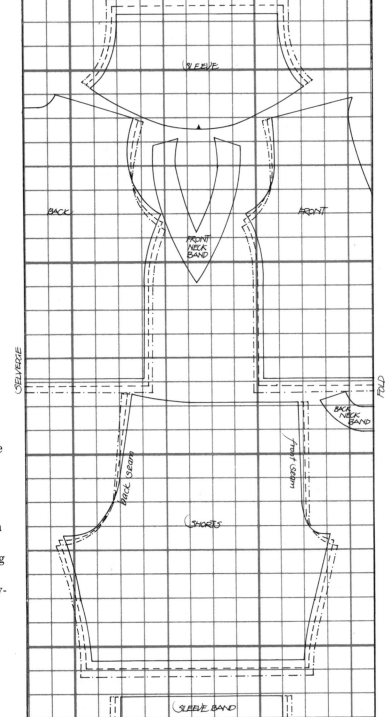

4 Lay pyjama top out flat, wrong side
   up, and pin right side of facing to
   wrong side of pyjama all round neck
   edge. Sew. Clip and trim seam
   allowance.
5 Turn facing through to right side of
   pyjama top and carefully press all
   round neck edge. Pin facing down
   and top stitch all round outside close
   to edge. Take out tacking and press.
6 Lay pyjama top out flat, with right
   side uppermost. With right sides
   together match sleeve top to
   shoulder seam, pin and sew sleeve in
   flat.
7 With right sides together, and taking
   care to match armhole seams, sew
   side and underarm seam in one, leaving 12cm (5in) unsewn at hem edge.
   Clip curves and press. Press back
   seam allowance at opening and top
   stitch round it. Repeat with second
   side.
8 Sleeve band: Take each band in
   turn. With right sides together, sew
   two short ends together to form a

circle and press. Turn a 1.5cm ($\frac{5}{8}$in) hem along one long edge, press and tack. Pin right side of unhemmed edge of band to wrong side of sleeve hem and sew. Press seam turning towards the band.

9 Turn band through to right side of sleeve, match tacked hem of band to previous stitching line. Pin and top stitch down. Press fold. Repeat with second sleeve.

10 Turn up hem as required.

Pyjama trousers

1 With right sides together, match the two trouser pieces. Sew centre front curving seam. Clip and press. Repeat with back seam.

2 With right sides together, and taking care to match centre front and back seams, sew inside leg seam in one. Clip curves and press.

3 Neaten waist edge then turn over a 3cm (1$\frac{1}{4}$in) hem and stitch, leaving a gap to insert elastic. Sew a line of top stitching close to fold edge at waist. This forms a neat casing.

4 Slot elastic through casing, adjust to fit and secure ends.

5 Hem trousers as required.

Nightie

A longer version of the pyjama top.

Variations

Quick-to-make pyjamas and nightie.
For summer: make them in fine cotton lawn, teaming the pyjama top with the bermudas.
For winter: make them in brushed cotton, extending the trouser pattern to make regular length pyjama trousers.

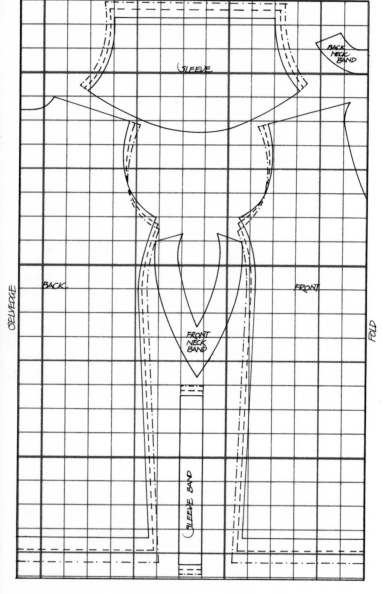

9 Pinafore skirt

A really tough bib-and-brace pinny skirt for school or play. Make it in something really strong like denim, and it'll be outgrown before it's out-worn.

Sizes: Shown in layout thus:
6-7 years ——
8-9 years - - - - -
10-11 years .-.-.-.

Fabric: *6-7 years:* 1.35m (1½yd) of 115cm (45in) wide fabric. *8-9 years:* 1.45m (1⅝yd) of 115cm (45in) wide fabric. *10-11 years:* 1.55m (1¾yd) of 115cm (45in) wide fabric.

Notions: 6 buttons, 2 × 10cm (4in) zips, 2 × 35mm (1½in) adjustable dungaree hooks.

1 Take bib pocket and mark fold. Fold flap over with right sides together and stitch a 1.5cm (⅝in) seam down each side of flap. Clip corners and turn flap through. Press fold.
2 Turn over and tack a 1.5cm (⅝in) hem all round rest of pocket. Position centrally on bib as indicated, pin and top stitch down all round close to edge.

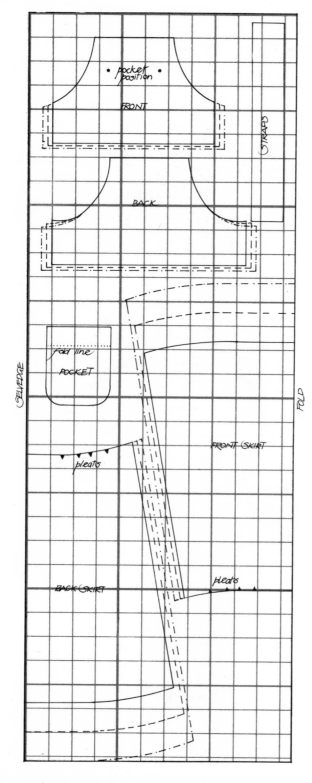

3 Take one strap section and turn a 1.5cm ($\frac{5}{8}$in) hem all round two long sides and one short. Top stitch all round the three sides. Press. Repeat on second strap.

4 Place the two front bib pieces on top of each other and, with right sides together, sew up left side, round left underarm curve, across top of bib, round right underarm curve and down right side. Clip corners and curves, trim seam allowance. Turn out and press. Bottom edges of bib are left free.

5 Place two back bib pieces on top of each other and, with right sides together, sew up both side seams and both curving underarm edges, leaving both top and bottom edges free.

6 Take the two straps and slip them between the two back sections. Sides of the straps should touch the curving seam, and raw edges of straps should be level with the raw edges of the bib top. Pin across the top of the bib and sew. Clip corners and curves. Turn bib out and press.

7 Take back and front skirt sections and, with right sides together, sew both side seams, finishing both seams 12cm (5in) away from waist edge. Press seams and press back the 1.5cm ($\frac{5}{8}$in) seam allowance at waist openings.

8 Take the two zips and pin and sew them into the openings.

9 Take the front bib and, with right sides together, pin the top (right side) layer of the bib to the skirt, matching bib ends to waist openings and centre front bib to centre front of skirt. Ease skirt on to bib by taking up the two marked pleats. Sew.

10 Press seam towards bib. Turn under a 1.5cm ($\frac{5}{8}$in) hem on underside of bib. Press and slip stitch to previous sewing line.

11 Repeat with back bib section, but

skirt openings are pinned and sewn starting 3.5cm (1½in) from sides of bib, to form flaps on which buttons are sewn. When slip stitchings the inside of bib, slip stitch to the ends of these flaps, to enclose seam turnings.

12 Mark and work the buttonholes, two on each side of front bib fairly close to the edge. Top stitch all round outside of both front and back bibs. Sew a button at each top corner of bib. Attach hooks to straps and secure.

13 Try the skirt on your child, slip straps over shoulders and secure hooks in correct position. Back flaps on bib slide under the front bib at sides. Mark position of buttons and sew on.

14 Turn up hem as required.

Variations
This little skirt needs to be made in strong fabric and clear, bright colours. Good fabrics would be denim, needlecord, drill or perhaps white piqué for summer.

30 Tee shirt and sweat shirt

Cotton knit tee and sweat shirts are ideal for holidays, weekends or sports. Knit them plain or give them zing with multi-coloured stripes.

A. TEE SHIRT

Yarn: Of No.3 cotton: 5 (6, 7) 50g balls, plus three shirt buttons.

Needles: A pair each of 2½mm (No.12) and 3mm (No.11).

Tension: 26 sts and 38 rows to 10cm (4in) square measured over st st on 3mm (No.11) needles.

Measurements: To fit ages 6-7 (8-9, 10-11): actual chest measurement 76(81,86) cm, 30(32,34)in; length 44(49,53)cm, 17(19½,21)in; sleeve seam 33(37,40)cm, 13(14½,16)in.
Instructions for larger sizes are in brackets.

Back
With 2½mm (No.12) needles cast on 97 (105, 111) sts and work 10 rows K1, P1 rib.
Change to 3mm (No.11) needles and cont in st st, comm with a K row.

Work 94 (108, 122) rows.
Shape armholes: Cast off 4 sts at beg of next 2 rows (89 (97, 103) sts).
Dec 1 st at beg of next and every following row until 75 (79, 81) sts rem.*
Cont without shaping until 166 (182, 200) rows have been worked from comm, ending with a P row.
Next row: Cast off 59 (61, 62) sts, K rem 16 (18, 19) sts.
Work 4 rows.
Next row: K (to form fold).
Work 8 rows comm with a K row.
Cast off.

Front
As back to *.
Cont without shaping until 140 (156, 174) rows have been worked from comm, ending with a P row.
Shape neck; Left side: Next row: K21 (23, 24), slip rem sts (54, 56, 57) on to a stitch holder.
Next row: P.
Next row: K.
Next row: P2 tog, P to end.

Repeat the last 2 rows four more times (16 (18, 19) sts).
Work 15 rows.
Next row: K (to form fold).
Work 4 rows comm with a K row.
Cast off.
Right side: Hold centre 33 sts on stitch holder, rejoin yarn to rem 21 (23, 24) sts and K to end.
Next row: P.
Next row: K2 tog, K to end.
Repeat the last 2 rows four more times (16 (18, 19) sts).
Work 15 rows.
Cast off.

Sleeves (2 alike)
With 2½mm (No.12) needles cast on 71 (77, 83) sts and work 10 rows K1, P1 rib.
Change to 3mm (No.11) needles, cont in st st comm with a K row.
Work 10 rows.
Shape sleeve head: Cast off 4 sts at beg of next two rows (63 (69, 75) sts).
6-7 and 8-9 year sizes only: Next row: K2 tog, K to end.
Next row: P2 tog, P to end.
Next row: K.
Next row: P.
Repeat the last 4 rows once more (59 (65) sts).
6-7 year size only: Repeat the last 4 rows once more (57 sts).
All sizes: Dec 1 st at beg of next and every following row until 27 sts rem.
Cast off.

Neckband
Join right shoulder seam. Fold back and sew down both hems of left shoulder opening.
With 2½mm (No.12) needle, and starting at fold of opening, pick up 50 sts across back neck, 18 sts down right side of neck, 33 sts across centre front, and 18 sts up left side of neck (119 sts).
Work 10 rows K1, P1 rib.
Cast off loosely in rib.

Make up

Follow pressing instructions on ball band. Join side and sleeve seams. Overlap left front opening and catch with a few stitches at armhole end. Sew sleeves into armholes. Make three buttonhole covered loops on front opening edge, and sew buttons on back edge to correspond.

B. SWEAT SHIRT

Yarn: Of No. 3 cotton 6 (7, 8) 50g balls.

Needles: A pair each of 2½mm (No.12) and 3mm (No.11).

Tension: 26 sts and 38 rows to 10cm (4in) square over st st on 3mm (No.11) needles.

Measurements: To fit ages 6-7 (8-9, 10-11): actual chest measurement 76(81,86) cm, 30(32,34)in; length 44(49,53)cm, 17½(19½,21)in; sleeve seam 33(37,40)cm, 13(14½,16)in.
Instructions for larger sizes are in brackets.

Back

With 2½mm (No.12) needles cast on 97 (105, 111) sts and work 10 rows K1, P1 rib.
Change to 3mm (No.11) needles and cont in st st, comm with a K row.
Work 94 (108, 122) rows.
Shape raglan: Cast off 4 sts at beg of next 2 rows (89 97, 103) sts).*
Next row: K2 tog, K to end.
Next row: P2 tog, P to end.
Next row: K.
Next row: P.
Repeat the last 4 rows eight (five, three) more times (71 (85, 95) sts).
Dec 1 st at beg of next and every following row until 45 sts rem.
Hold on a stitch holder.

Front

As back to *.
Dec 1 st at beg of next and every following row until 57 (69, 77) sts rem.
8-9 and 10-11 year sizes only: Dec 1 st at beg and end of next and every following row until 57 (57) sts rem.
All sizes: Divide for neck: Left side:
Next row: K11, slip rem sts (46) on to a stitch holder.
Dec 1 st at beg of next and every following row until 2 sts rem.
Cast off.
Right side: Hold centre 35 sts on stitch holder, rejoin yarn to rem 11 sts and K2 tog, K to end.
Dec 1 st at beg of next and every following row until 2 sts rem.
Cast off.

Right sleeve

With 2½mm (No.12) needles cast on 53 (55, 57) sts and work 10 rows K1, P1 rib.
Change to 3mm (No.11) needles and cont in st st, comm with a K row.
Inc 1 st at beg and end of next and every following 10th row until there are 73 (79, 85) sts on the needle.
Cont without shaping until 124 (138, 152) rows have been worked from comm, ending with a P row.
Shape raglan: Cast off 4 sts at beg of next 2 rows (65 (71, 77) sts).
Dec 1 st at beg of next and every following row until 31 (39, 47) sts rem.
Dec 1 st at beg and end of next and every following row until 15 sts rem, ending with a P row.*
Next row: Cast off 4 sts, K to end.
Next row: P.
Next row: K.
Next row: P2 tog, P to end.
Next row: K2 tog, K to end.
Repeat the last 4 rows until 2 sts rem.
Cast off.

Left sleeve

As right sleeve to *.
Next row: K.
Next row: Cast off 4 sts, P to end.
Next row: K.
Next row: P.
Next row: K2 tog, K to end.
Next row: P2 tog, P to end.
Repeat the last 4 rows until 2 sts rem.
Cast off.

Neckband

Join raglan seams, leaving right back
seam open. With 2½mm (No.12) needle
pick up 18 sts from right sleeve top, 48
sts from front neck, 18 sts from left
sleeve top, and 45 sts across back neck
(129 sts).
Work 10 rows K1, P1 rib.
Cast off loosely in rib.

Make up

Follow pressing instructions on ball
band. Join raglan seam and neckband.
Join side and sleeve seams.

Variations

Spend those gloomy winter evenings
knitting these for sunny days ahead.
Thin stripes of zingy colour look best,
and make the knitting that much more
interesting.

31 Track suit

For the jogger in your family. Great for sports at school or dashing around at weekends. In waterproof fabric it would be excellent for bad-weather cycling, fishing or camping.

Sizes: Shown on layout thus:
6-7 years ———
8-9 years - - - - -
10-11 years ·--··--· ·

Fabric: 2.20m (2½yd) of 140cm (55in) wide track-suit fabric. Piece of interfacing for collar.

Notions: 44, 46 or 48cm (17, 18 or 19in) open-ended zip, braid for stripes, cord for hem, narrow elastic and waistband elastic.

Before you start: Cut collar piece out in interfacing.

Jacket

1 Take pocket piece and turn a 1.5cm (⅝in) hem all round. Sew a line of top stitching 1cm (½in) away from edge all round pocket. Pin pocket to jacket front at desired height from hem, with straight edge of pocket parallel with side of jacket and 3cm (1¼in) away from side of jacket. Top stitch pocket all round curved edge. Repeat with second pocket.

and press. Repeat with second sleeve
and jacket back.

6 With right sides together, and taking
care to match armhole seams, sew
underarm and side seams in one.
Clip curve and press.

7 Neaten jacket hem edge by turning
under a tiny hem and sew. Then turn
up and sew a 2cm ($\frac{3}{4}$in) hem. Stitch
and press.

2 Take the two front pieces and fold
back a 1.5cm ($\frac{5}{8}$in) turning down
both centre front edges, press. Open
zip, place zip sections right side up
under front edges, starting 2cm (1in)
from top edge and having turned
under taped edges of zip at top. Tack
and sew in place. Check that zip runs
smoothly and that top and bottom
match.

3 Take sleeve and, with right sides
together, pin and sew dart. Press
open. Position braid for stripes as
desired and top stitch close to top
and bottom edge. Repeat for second
sleeve.

4 With right sides together, match
points A and B on jacket front and
points A and B on sleeve front and
sew between the two points. Clip
curve and press. Repeat with second
front and second sleeve.

5 With right sides together match
points C and D on jacket back with
points C and D on sleeve back and
sew between two points. Clip curve

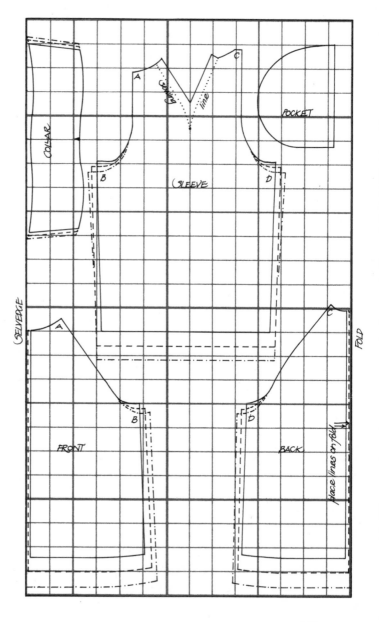

8 Neaten sleeve hems by turning up a tiny hem and sewing. Turn up a 2cm ($\frac{3}{4}$in) hem and stitch round leaving a small gap to insert elastic. Top stitch all round sleeve hem close to fold.

9 Insert elastic, adjust to fit and secure.

10 Take one collar piece and tack interfacing to wrong side. Place second collar piece over it and, with right sides together, sew all round three sides, leaving bottom edges free. Trim seam allowance to 6mm ($\frac{1}{4}$in), turn collar out and press.

11 Take one free edge of collar and, with right sides together, match centre back of collar to centre back of jacket. Pin collar edge to jacket, matching collar ends to centre front openings of jacket. Sew.

12 Press collar away from jacket. Clip and trim seam allowance. Turn a 1.5cm ($\frac{5}{8}$in) hem under on remaining raw edge of collar. Slip stitch to inside of jacket neck following previous stitching line.

13 Run cord through hem, knot ends and tie.

Trousers

1 Mark lines for side stripes with chalk or tacking. Pin on braid and top stitch close to edges.

2 Construct trousers in same way as pyjama trousers on page 102. But turn up hems, leaving a gap to insert elastic. Thread elastic through. Adjust to fit and secure ends.

Variations

The jogging suit – every kid seems to want one. The jacket can be made in any fabric. It's a really simple pattern, so why not make a couple for your little athlete?

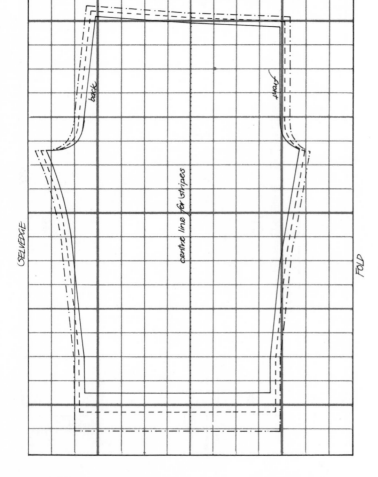

32 Zip coat

Only minimal sewing on this marvellous coat for both girls and boys. Big, roomy hood to keep out winter chills. Lovely big pockets to carry all those vital bits and bobs.

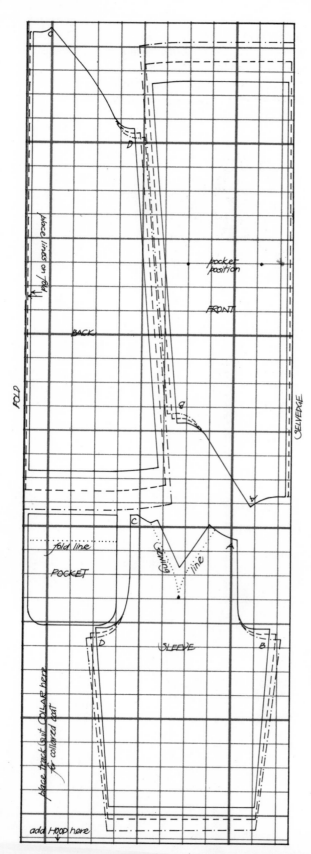

On the pattern layout, text labels read:

place lines on top of coat

FOLD

BACK

pocket position

FRONT

SELVEDGE

fold line

POCKET

guide line

place track (suit COLLAR here for collared coat

SLEEVE

add HOOD here

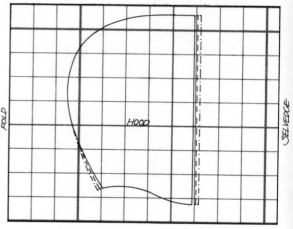

FOLD

HOOD

SELVEDGE

Sizes: Shown on layout thus:
6-7 years ——
8-9 years - - - - -
10-11 years -·-·-·-

Fabric: *Hooded coat:* 2.15m (2⅜yd) of 115cm (45in) wide fabric. *Collared version:* 1.70m (1⅞yd) of 115cm (45in) wide fabric.

Notions: 62cm (25in) open-ended zip, matching thread.

1. Take pocket piece and mark fold. Fold over flap with right sides together and stitch a 1.5cm (⅝in) seam down each side of flap. Clip corners and turn flap through, press fold.
2. Turn over and tack a 1.5cm (⅝in) hem all round rest of pocket. Position on coat, pin and top stitch all round close to edge. Repeat with second pocket if desired.
3. Take hood pieces and, with right sides together, sew a 2cm (¾in) seam around curving back edge. Fell this seam (see 'How To' guide, page 122). Press.
4. Take sleeve and, with right sides together, pin and sew dart. Press open. Repeat with second sleeve.

5 With right sides together, match points A and B on coat front with points A and B on sleeve front. Sew between these points. Clip curve and press. Repeat with second front and sleeve.

6 With right sides together, match points C and D on coat back with points C and D on sleeve back. Sew between these points. Clip curve and press. Repeat on second sleeve and back.

7 Take hood and, with right sides together, taking care to match centre back of hood with centre back of coat, pin hood to coat neckline, ensuring hood edges are matching coat fronts exactly. Sew.

8 Press seam allowance towards coat, trim the under seam to 6mm ($\frac{1}{4}$in), turn under the raw edge of upper seam allowance, tack and top stitch down. Pull out tacking and press.

9 Neaten hood front edges by turning a tiny hem and stitching down. Then turn under and tack down a 1.5cm ($\frac{5}{8}$in) turning all round hood front edges.

10 Open zip and turn back the taped ends at top; slip stitch down. Place zip sections right side up under front edges starting 1.5cm ($\frac{5}{8}$in) down from neck seam. Tack in place, and make sure zip closes easily.

11 Now sew zip in on left side of coat and continue the stitching around the hood and down the right side of coat sewing in zip on that side also.

12 With right sides together and taking care to match armhole seams, sew underarm seams and side seams in one. Clip curve and press.

13 Turn up sleeve hems as required and hem by hand. Press.

14 Turn up hem as desired.

Variations
This coat is basically the same construction as the track suit (No.31). If you don't want a hood you can use the collar pattern from the track suit and attach it in the same way.

33 Kids' bags

Children seem to carry so much around in their pockets, why not help them out a bit and make them one of these bags?

1 A duffle bag – great for swimming or sports gear. Make it in ciré to stand up to damp swimming togs.
2 Back packs are really good for carrying books to and from school – no more dragging scruffy carrier bags along the street, and the webbing straps really do take the strain. Far safer, too, than hanging bags from bike handlebars if your child cycles to school.
3 For gym and ballet shoes a simple drawstring bag is ideal. Make it in a bright colour, or embroider your child's name across it for instant recognition at school.

1 Take rectangle of fabric and, with right sides together, sew long side seam (this forms a tube). Press seam open.
2 Take loop section, fold in half lengthways and sew up long side. Trim seam and turn through. Press and fold in half to form loop. Tack.
3 With right sides together, pin one circular base into one end of the tube. Take the tacked loop and pin in position along this seam in base, level with side seam. Sew in base. Turn right side out.
4 Cut 24cm (9½in) circle of card. Take second circle of fabric and glue to cardboard, glueing seam allowance under too. Allow to dry thoroughly.
5 Neaten top edge of bag and fold over a 5cm (2in) hem and stitch down. Mark position of 8 eyelets 2.5cm (1in) down from top and evenly spaced around it. Attach eyelets according to manufacturer's instructions.
6 Take slide section, fold in half lengthways and sew down long side. Trim seam and turn through. Press. Sew two short ends to each other to

DUFFLE BAG

Fabric: 60cm (24in) of 90cm (36in) wide fabric.

Notions: Eight large eyelets. 1m (1yd) of cord. Some stiff card. Fabric glue.

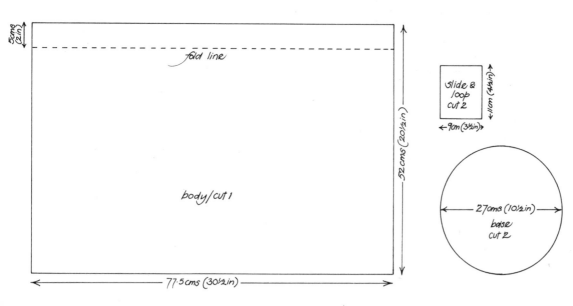

form a circle and press, with this seam in the centre. Stitch along the seam through both layers of material to form two channels.

7 Starting and ending with the eyelets at each side of the side seam, slot cord through all the eyelets in turn. Take loose ends of cord and slot through channels on slide, then through loop at base. Knot. Draw up cord and push up slide.

BACK PACK

Fabric: 50cm (20in) of 90cm (36in) wide fabric.

Notions: Bias binding, 1m (1yd) of 4cm (1½in) wide webbing, one large toggle button.

1 Mark fold lines on main piece with tacking. Mark strap and pocket position.
2 Bind front edge.
3 Bind curved flap.
4 Bind top of side panels.
5 Take the two pieces of webbing 50cm (20in) long and attach, as Figures 1 and 2.

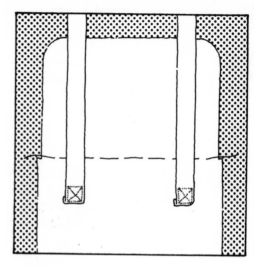

figure 1

6 Take pocket piece. Turn under 2.5cm (1in) hem and stitch down along one long edge.
7 Turn under 1.5cm (⅝in) hem and tack all round three remaining sides. Position pocket and top stitch down. Machine divisions as required.
8 Using tacked fold lines as a guide, and with right sides together, sew in side panels. Turn right side out and press.
9 Stiffen base with a piece of card cut to correct size.

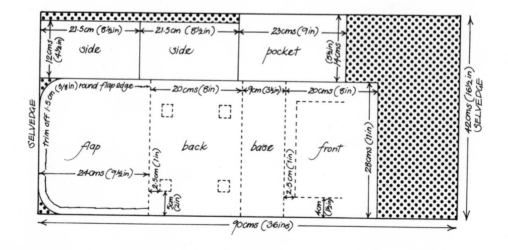

118

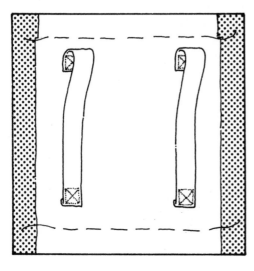

 figure 2

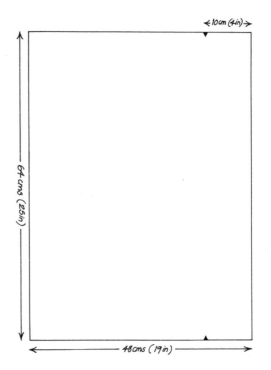

10 Take a piece of bias tape 8cm (3in)
long, fold in half lengthways and
stitch through. Fold in half to form a
loop and slip stitch to the underside
of the flap at the centre front. Sew
toggle to front and fasten.

BALLET OR GYM SHOE BAG

Fabric: 50cm (20in) of 90cm (36in)
wide fabric.

Notions: Cord for drawstring – 1m (1yd)

1 Cut out pattern in fabric.
2 With right sides together, fold
rectangle in half and sew across short
end.
3 Sew long side seam to notch. Press
back seam allowance at opening.
4 Neaten top edge and then fold over a
2cm (¾in) hem. Stitch down close to
edge. Turn out and press.
5 Slot cord through casing and knot.
Draw up.

'How to' Guide

2 By hand, oversew along raw edges.

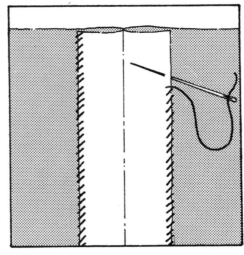

Neatening edges
When using fabrics that fray, it is worthwhile spending a little time neatening the seam turnings. Here are three ways:

1 If you have a swing-needle machine, zig-zag close to or slightly over the edge.

3 Use pinking shears when cutting out or trimming seam allowances.

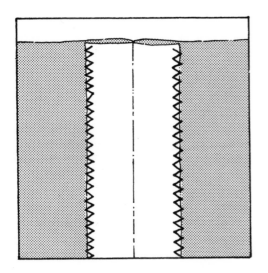

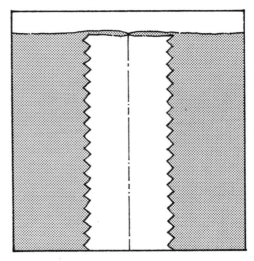

Felled seam

This is a very strong seam which is also useful as it needs no neatening and is easier than a french seam to work. Sew seam in usual way but press both seam allowances to one side. Trim away only the under seam, turn under top seam and press and top stitch down to conceal trimmed edge. This seam also looks effective on fine fabrics.

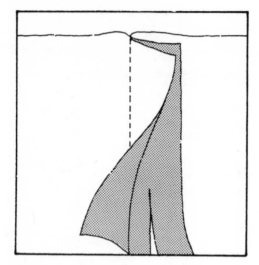

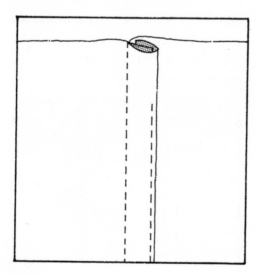

Pressing

To give any garment a professional finish, it is essential to press every seam as it is sewn. Use a large piece of muslin dipped in water and wrung out as tightly as possible. Press on the wrong side of the fabric only.

Shirring

Shirring is very simple indeed. Take the shirring elastic and wind it onto the sewing machine spool by hand, Put the spool into the machine in the usual way. Thread the top part of the machine in the usual way. Set stitch length to the longest stitch. Keep the right side of the fabric uppermost.

Clipping curves

When a seam is curved, trim away excess allowance after sewing and clip with scissors, towards but not too close to seam. Then press.

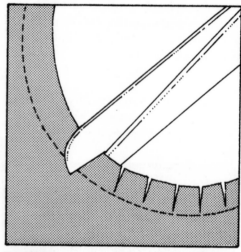

Binding

A neat way to finish off any kind of raw edge. The following instructions are for binding a neck or armhole where the edges are curved. Straight edges are worked in the same way, but they're easier.

Take the bias binding and open out one edge. Place this edge right sides together, and pin against the edge of the garment neck, slightly stretching the binding as you go round the curves. Stitch down along fold (leaving 1.5cm ($\frac{5}{8}$in) of bias binding extra at centre back neck). Press excess 1.5cm ($\frac{5}{8}$in) of binding under, to wrong side. Fold rest of binding to inside neck with the fold edge just covering the previous line of stitching. Tack down. Turn to right side and top stitch in the dip between the bias and the fabric of the garment. (If you use matching thread this stitch line will disappear.) Slip stitch centre back join.

Stitching a curved hem

Stitch all round hem 6mm ($\frac{1}{4}$in) away from the edge. On the curved part of the hem pull these stitches up slightly to take up excess fabric. Turn over a tiny hem along stitch line and then another hem the required amount. Stitch down using herringbone or slip stitch. Press using a damp cloth; this will 'shrink' the gathering into place.

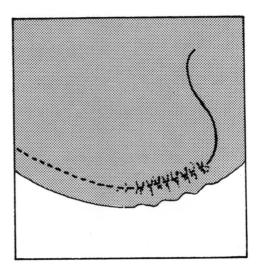

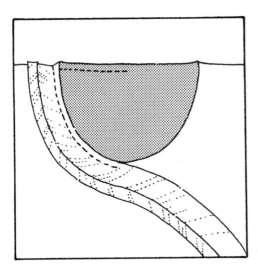

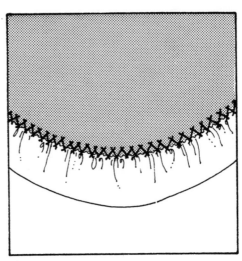

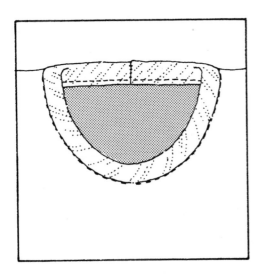

Appliqué (Duvet covers page 32)
Sketch out the design lightly on to the
background fabric. Trace off each
individual shape, cut out in fabric, iron
interfacing on to wrong side. Position
shape in place and tack down. Work a
close zig-zag stitch round edge of shape.
Pull out tacking.

Chain stitch (Duvet covers page 32)
To work chain stitch, bring the needle
through to right side. Then, holding the
cotton down with the left thumb, put
the needle in beside the point where it
came out. Take up a tiny stitch, draw
the cotton through the loop made by
holding the cotton down with the
thumb. Put the needle in again beside
the last stitch and continue.

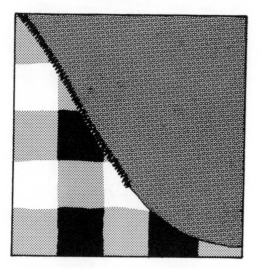

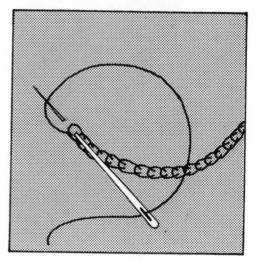

Yarn Brand names and manufacturers

No. 1	Teddy Bear push chair suit	– Sirdar Pullman
No. 4	Baby sweater, hat and mitts	– Twilleys Stalite
No. 10	Waistcoat	– Sirdar Country Style Double Knitting
No. 12	Face sweater	– Sirdar Country Style Double Knitting
No. 14	Monogram jacket	– Sirdar Pullman
No. 16	Tee shirt and sweat shirt	– Twilleys Stalite
No. 18	Knit-and-quilt coat	– Sirdar Pullman
No. 21	Bobble hats and scarves	– Sirdar Country Style Double Knitting
No. 23	Ski sweater	– Patons Capstan
No. 26	Chunky-knit jacket	– Patons Husky
No. 30	Tee shirt and sweat shirt	– Twilleys Stalite

Sirdar:
Sirdar Ltd,
P.O. Box 31,
Alverthorpe,
Wakefield,
Yorkshire.

Twilleys:
H. G. Twilley Ltd,
Roman Mill,
Stamford,
Lincs.

Patons:
Paton and Baldwin Ltd,
P.O. Box 28,
Macmullen Road,
Darlington, DL1 1YQ
Co. Durham.

Acknowledgements

The authors acknowledge the help they received from H. W. Peel & Company Limited who supplied the 'True Sew' pattern paper used for making up the garments throughout this book. Details of local suppliers can be obtained from the manufacturers H. W. Peel & Company Limited at Jeymer Drive, Greenford, Middx.

Fabrics used for colour photographs
1 Babies' blue duck print dungies, opposite page 33: Viyella (55% wool, 45% cotton).
2 Red harem trousers and navy gathered skirt (worn with face sweaters), opposite page 48: Viyella (55% wool, 45% cotton).
3 Blue-printed play dungarees and sun suit, opposite page 49: 100% cotton by Laura Ashley.
4 Tartan dressing gown and navy blue pyjamas, opposite page 81: Viyella (55% wool, 45% cotton).
5 Cream blouse with red spots (worn with denim skirt), opposite page 96: Viyella (55% wool, 45% cotton).

All shoes kindly loaned by Start-Rite.